How to use DEPTH SOUNDERS & GPS

FRED STUDDEN

I0792562

How to use Depth Sounders & GPS

FRED STUDDEN

AFN
AUSTRALIAN FISHING NETWORK

First published in 2008
Published and distributed by
Australian Fishing Network
Unit 19 & 20, 1 Clare Street
Bayswater, VIC 3153
Ph: +61 3 9729 8788
Fax: +61 3 9729 7833
Email: sales@afn.com.au
Website: www.afn.com.au
Email: sales@afn.com.au
Website: www.afn.com.au

Ilustrations by Fred Studden.
Additional Illustrations by Trevor Hawkins.

ISBN 9781 8651 3152 8

ACKNOWLEDGEMENTS

There are some many skilful and clever people, some technical and some fishermen both professional and recreational, who taught me so much and, without their help over the years, I would not have had the knowledge or the incentive to put this book together. While it is impossible to name all, to them I owe a great debt of gratitude and thanks.

I would like to thank numerous people who have help in the preparation of this work, they include, David Maitland (Furuno), Estelle Baldery (Lowrance), Robin Kidde and his crew (Oceantalk) Mick Gregory and Tim Morgan (Humminbird), Peter Langbart (GME) and Richard Cummings.

Many thanks to the people at AFN, who have shown remarkable patience and understanding, without which the book would never have become anything other than a collection of computer printouts.

Special thanks to my fishing mate, Ian Croft, who made his boat, Assassin, available, not only for fishing trips but also, as a test bed for numerous sounders and plotters.

To my wife of 50 years, Yvonne, who has shared my love of fishing and with whom I have fished every spare minute we have had available, mainly offshore but these days more and more in the freshwater scene, go my heartfelt thanks and love. Yvonne has proof read and corrected all the text and captions and, without complaint, has put up with all the time I spent with the computer or out on the water, neglecting all those household jobs.

CONTENTS

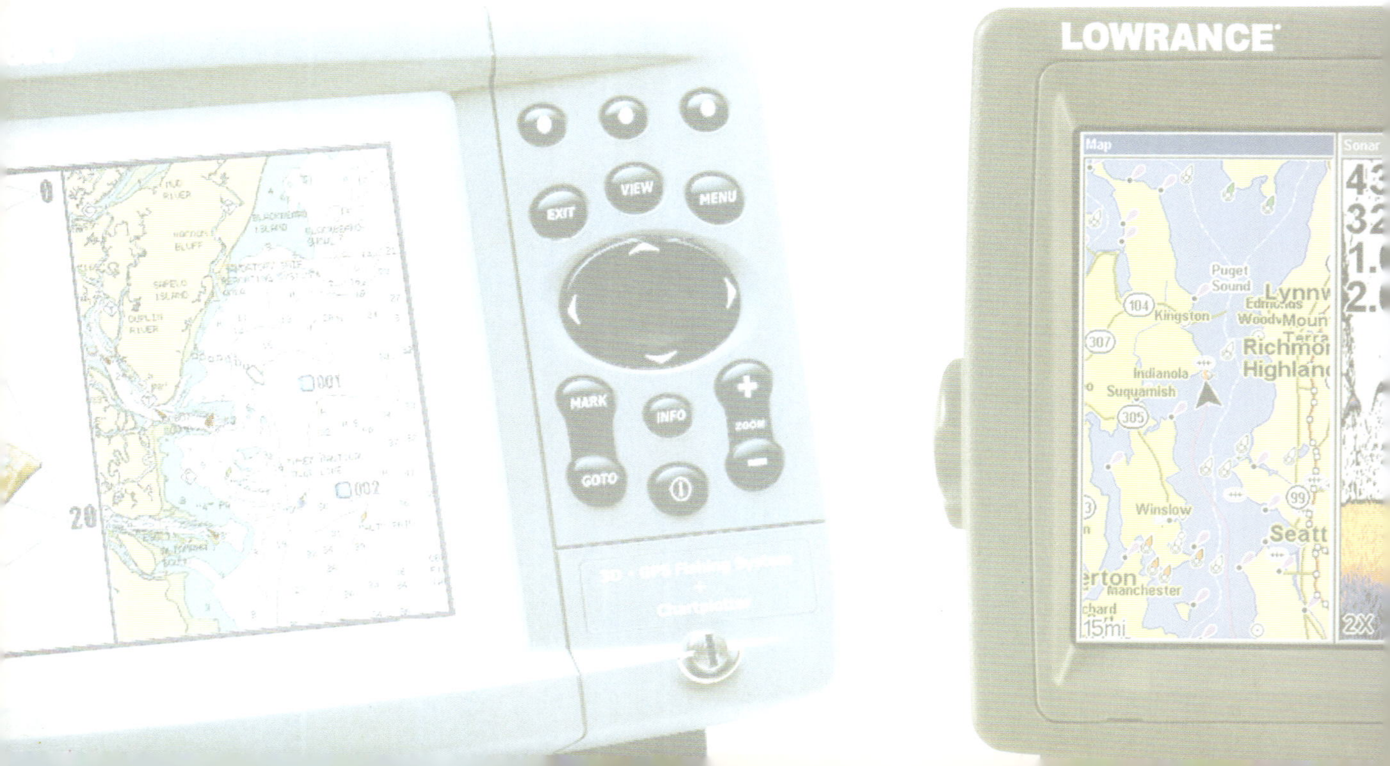

LOWRANCE
EXIT
VIEW
MENU
MARK
INFO
ZOOM
GOTO
Map
Sonar
Puget Sound
Kingston
Indianola
Suquamish
Winslow
Manchester

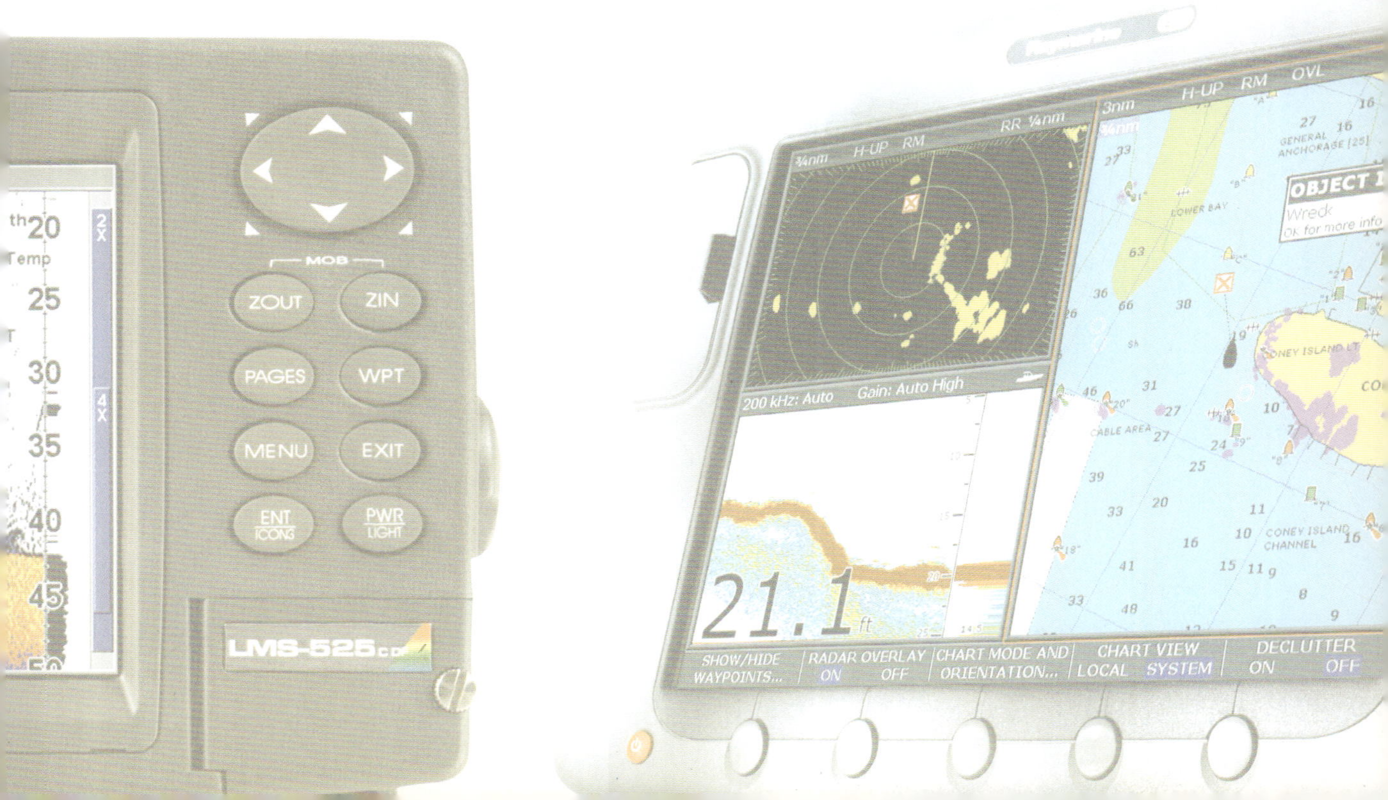

MOB
ZOUT
ZIN
PAGES
WPT
MENU
EXIT
ENT ICONS
PWR LIGHT
LMS-525
H-UP RM
200 kHz: Auto
Gain: Auto High
21.1 ft
SHOW/HIDE WAYPOINTS...
RADAR OVERLAY ON OFF
CHART MODE AND ORIENTATION...
CHART VIEW LOCAL SYSTEM
DECLUTTER ON OFF

The Author with a mulloway taken in Lake Macquarie.

Introduction

Since the 1990s when the Global Positioning System first became fully available to recreational boaters, there have been incredible advances made in the design and production in this arena, and today's units have a degree of sophistication undreamed of even a decade ago. Due to the advances made in mass production technology of electronic equipment and the huge worldwide market for GPS and sounders, the cost in real terms of these units has fallen considerably. Modern units are cheaper than they have ever been—yet have more features and facilities than ever before.

As a result of these technological advantages, there would be few serious recreational fishing boats not equipped with a GPS receiver and a depth sounder, and yet to many users this equipment represents 'black box' technology and its use is still shrouded in mystery. Due to this attitude, many owners are not realising anywhere near the full potential of their equipment and others are reluctant to purchase new gear because of the fear they may not be able to use it properly.

I hope this book will assist all users of sounders and GPS to better understand their equipment and thus obtain improved performance and results. Also, for those who are contemplating buying their first unit, an understanding of the basic concepts will make their choice more informed and ultimately help them to select the model best for their individual needs.

I am also a keen angler, fishing mainly offshore for most of my life, and regularly use all types of marine electronics, giving me the unique advantage of understanding both the technical and practical side of the equipment described in this book. I have kept the text, wherever possible, to a non-technical level, only straying into specialised terminology when essential to understand an important point of the operation of the equipment.

I have tried to make the book's appeal universal by keeping descriptions and examples as generic as possible and, while there are a number of brands mentioned, the theory of operation and various specifications has been kept as non-specific as possible. On occasions, when particular brands may be mentioned, it is to draw attention to a special feature or function and is not intended as a personal recommendation of any one brand.

Wherever possible illustrations have been used to show readers what to expect from their units. All of the screen images are downloads of actual on-the-water performance, the earlier black and white images were made using the Lowrance Snapshot program and the colour illustrations using Navman's Navision. Both of these programs downloaded and saved the screen images to a laptop computer. Today the images were saved using internal memory cards on Humminbird, Lowrance and Raymarine equipment.

Finally, while it is virtually impossible to predict what the future holds for marine electronics with any degree of certainly, one can be assured there will be continued improvements of existing systems and innovations will constantly appear on the market. I am sure the next 50 years will be as exciting as the last 50.

FRED STUDDEN

Part one
Depth Sounders

Chapter one
Sounder History

EARLY DAYS

For as long as mariners have been going to sea they have needed to determined the depth of water beneath their boat's keel. The original method was to use a weight on the end of a long line. The weight was dropped to the bottom and the depth was read from coloured markers attached to the line. This was know as 'sounding' the depth and the line was known, not surprisingly as a 'sounding line or a lead line'. This manual sounding method worked well in relatively shallow water but as the depth increased this became a laborious task and was only effective when the boat was moving slowly.

In the 1870s a more accurate method for deep water soundings was developed for the Royal Navy. This consisted of a glass tube sealed at the top and the inside was coated with a chemical that changed colour when wet. The tube was encased in a robust brass tube open to the surrounding water and lowered on a wire cable to the bottom. As the device descended in the water column, the increasing pressure compressed the air at the top of the tube allowing water to enter the bottom. When the wire became slack, indicating the bottom had been reached, the device was recovered and the changed colour on the inside of the glass indicated the amount of air compression that was then converted to indicate the water depth. This was also a slow, laborious job and it became obvious a mechanical method was needed.

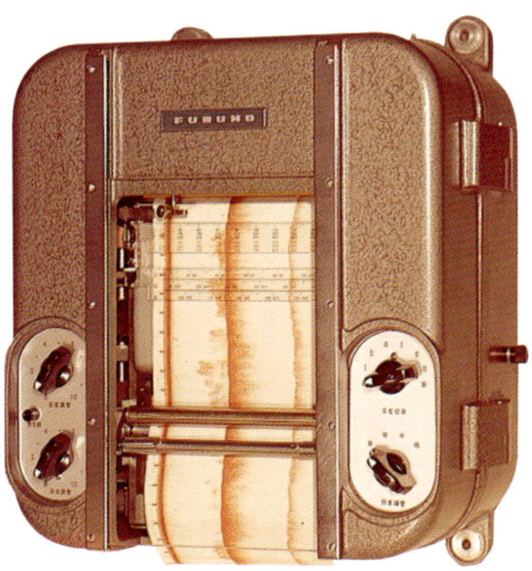

(Fig 1) Early sounders
The F216C was Furuno's first sounder introduced in 1946 and is probably the first successful paper sounder produced specifically for the commercial fishing trade.

(Fig 2) Lowrance Fish-Lo-K-Tor
This is the sounder that established Lowrance as one of the World's leading sounder manufacturers, the 'little green box', the Fish-Lo-K-Tor. Produced in 1959, the Fish-Lo-K-Tor was a flasher only sounder that operated from internal dry cells and became instantly popular with fishermen the World over. This was the first sounder produced for the recreational fishermen and sold over one million units.

In the 1930s American engineers developed the first hydrophone. This consisted of an electrically operated hammer striking a metal diaphragm at a rate of three blows per second. The diaphragm was mounted in a tube open to the sea in the bottom of the ship's hull. A separate diaphragm in the hull received the returning echoes and converted these into electrical pulses. The operator listened to the electrical pulses on earphones and by constantly tuning the receiver and referring to a predetermined scale, the operator was able to read the depth. This was a vast improvement on the lead line sounding. However, the operator's ear fatigue was a problem which, in 1937, lead to the operator being replaced by a paper recording device that produced surprisingly detailed pictures of the bottom considering this type of machine was operating at audio frequencies. Thus the first echo sounder was born.

At about the same, time in the United Kingdom, an ultrasonic sounding machine was being developed that generated pulses using a number of thin metal plates pulsed by a powerful magnetic field. When these units came into service it was noticed there were often echoes recorded above the sea bed. These were quickly recognised as reflections from fish schools, and thus the fishfinder was born.

(Fig 4) *Lowrance X-15*

(Fig 3 & Fig 4) Classic graph sounders
The Furuno FE400 and the Lowrance X-15 were both very popular sounders of the paper graph era. The FE400 was a simple, reliable and robust unit with phased depth ranges. The X-15 was the first recreational graph unit to use a microprocessor to control the various features of the sounder and, together with the X-16, epitomised graph paper sounders at the peak of their development.

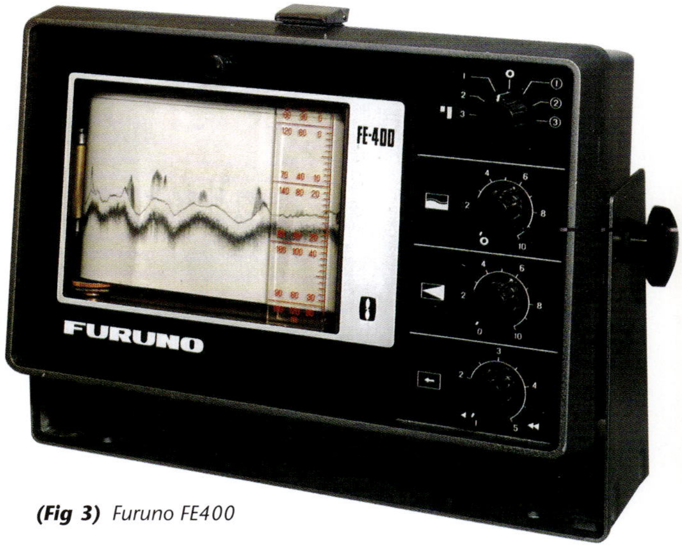

(Fig 3) *Furuno FE400*

SOUNDER DEVELOPMENT

These early sounders were both large and expensive. Developments and improvements from WWII and the introduction of transistors, integrated circuits and piezoceramic transducers in the late 1950s brought both the size and cost of sounders to the affordable level for recreational sports fishermen. (Fig 1)

The first of these 'sports sounder' used a rotating disk mounted in a case with a rotary scale marked in water depths. A small neon tube was fitted to the edge of the disk, which emitted a flash as a surface mark and then flashed when the returning echo was received. Since the disk had rotated some way between the surface flash and receiving and displaying the bottom echo, the distance between the surface mark and the bottom echo, and thus the depth, could be read from the scale. Due to the rapid rotation of the disk the flashes appeared to be stationary. Fish echoes also appeared as somewhat weaker flashes above the bottom. This sounder is know as 'flasher', or 'rotary flashers' Experienced operators became very skilled and were able to glean a great deal of information—information such as bottom hardness and fish species—from what, by present standards, was a very simple device.
(Fig 2)

The next improvement was fitting a stylus, or 'pen', to the disk which 'etched' a record of each flash on a slowly advancing role of special paper. Because the 'picture' was drawn as part of a circle, his type of graph is known as a 'curvilinear' trace. As the graph paper was an ongoing expense, many of the rotary sounders incorporated a facility to turn the graph paper off and only use the flashing display. This type of sounder is known as a 'flasher-graph'.

The next evolution was fitting the stylus to a belt that moved vertically from the top to the bottom of the graph paper, producing an undistorted image. These sounders are called 'straight line' graphs and reached the zenith of their development with the hugely successful 'X-15' from Lowrance in the USA. (Fig 3)(Fig 4) These units were capable of incredible detail that has only been equalled in the last few years by LCD units.

When the first LCD (Liquid Crystal Displays) appeared on the market, few could have foreseen the impact this style of sounder would have. The first units' displays were 'blocky' and of relatively low contrast, however even these first sounders showed glimpses of the features that have made all other types obsolete except for specialised applications. The LCD system is fully explored in other chapters of this book.

(Fig 5) State of the art LCD colour sounder
Raymarine's E80, a modern, large screen colour LCD display.

Video sounder development has run parallel with paper graph and LCD unit development. Video machines use a Cathode Ray Tube (CRT), similar to the domestic TV sets of the 1990s, to display the echoes. For many years this type of unit was the only viable colour echo sounder available and was much favoured by commercial operators. However, they had several inherent characteristics that made them unsuitable for the average sportfishing boat, except for the keenest fishermen, usually game fishing enthusiasts fishing deep water from larger boats. Today the large screen LCD displays are becoming increasingly popular for this type of application. (Fig 5)

Video units usually are large—the cathode ray tube is itself a bulky item. Large displays have the advantage of being viewable from some distance away, a plus when used on big boats, however this feature also makes them unsuitable for installing in small, open boats. The video display was also difficult to see in bright light, impossible in sunlight. These types of sounders also generate considerable amounts of heat and some ventilation of the components is necessary, making the case difficult if not impossible to fully waterproof, another major disadvantage for small boat operation.

A characteristic of video displays is that high voltages are required to drive the tube—high voltage and a damp environment are a sure recipe for trouble, not a desirable feature. Also, large amounts of current were drawn by this type of unit, anything from a couple of amps for the smaller sized sounders to four or even five amps for the larger sets.

The rapid developments within the computer industry of large, bright, high definition colour LCD screens has flowed onto the sounder markets and this type of display has all but replaced the video display sounders. These later generation colour screens are true daylight viewable, even in direct sunlight with little or no 'washing-out' of the colour. Unlike the cathode ray tubes that require a deep housing, the LCD screens are thin, only six or seven millimetres or even less in many cases. Colour LCD display screens consume very little current and produce no heat, making waterproof housings practical.

The colour LCD sounder is still considerably more costly than the monochrome (black and white) units, however the price is steadily falling and the future of sounders seems to be heading towards full colour units, in fact one major manufacturer, Raymarine, no longer produces monochrome sounders.

The terms, 'Echo Sounder', 'Sounder', 'Sonar' and 'Fishfinder' all refer to the same device. In the USA, the terms fishfinder and sonar are commonly used, while in Australia and the UK, sounder, depth sounder and echo sounder are generally the most common definitions, although fishfinder is becoming more acceptable these days. The simple term 'sounder' is used throughout the book to describe these devices.

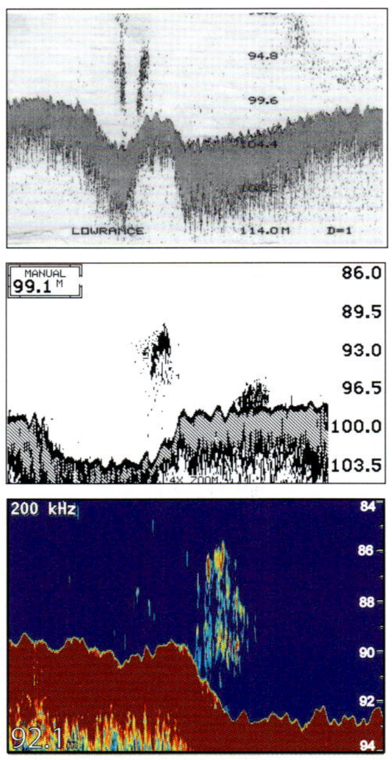

Lowrance X-15A graph sounder 1982

Lowrance LMS 350a monochrome LCD sounder 1989

Raymarine A65 colour LCD sounder 2007

(Fig 6)
Comparison of past and present sounder images
The three images graphically illustrate the improvements in sounder technology through the years. All of these soundings were made within about half a mile of each, other although separated by over 25 years. The area is locally known as 'the farm' about 12 miles off Swansea on the NSW coast.

Chapter two

Sounder Basics

The previous chapters described some of the history of sounders and touched on the basic types of displays, the next few chapters will go into some basic details on how sounders operate and more 'in-depth' description of sounder types. These basics are generic and are common to all types and brands of sounders.

The basic components of all sounders, regardless of their type or application, consist of four main components, the transmitter, transducer, receiver and the display. (Fig 7) The transmitter produces pulses of electrical energy that is passed on to the transducer, which converts the electrical energy to sound pulses that are directed into the water. If these pulses strike an object in the water column, an echo is reflected back to the transducer, which converts this sonic echo pulse into electrical energy. This energy is of a very low level and is amplified by the receiver and then displayed for the user.

While the basic principles remain the same, subtle variations are made to the operating parameters depending on the tasks the sounder is intended to handle or on a particular manufacturer's views on what attributes are needed to make the 'perfect' sounder. Some of the parameters commonly varied are, frequency of the output pulse, the output power of the unit, the angle of the sound pulse and the method of displaying the returning echo.

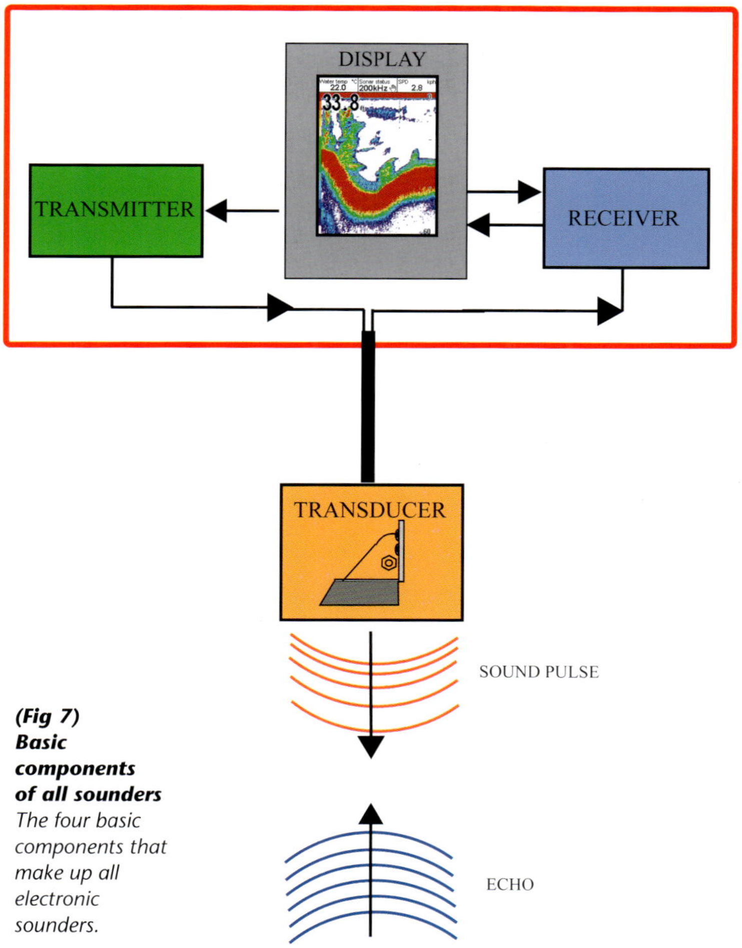

(Fig 7) Basic components of all sounders
The four basic components that make up all electronic sounders.

Sound waves travel at a fixed rate in water, about 1460 metres per second (4,800 ft/sec). The length of time taken for the pulse to travel from the transducer to the bottom and back to the transducer enables the distance from the boat to the bottom—the depth—to be calculated.

While the speed of sound in water is fixed, the rate at which the sound's power is absorbed by the water is related to the frequency of the pulse, the higher the frequency, the greater the absorption. Common frequencies used in recreational sounders are 400, 200 and 50 kilohertz. The frequency of the pulse also plays a significant part in the resolution of the echo, with the high frequencies—those absorbed best by the water—producing the greatest resolution. Resolution is the capability of the sounder to separate and display small echoes as separate targets.

While there are sounders available that simply display the water depth—usually in large digital numbers—these are mainly used for navigation rather than for fishing applications. As the returning echoes contain vastly more information than just the water depth, a graphic display is used to display the echoes in a meaningful way to show the bottom profile, the depth of water and any fish that may be present below the boat.

(Fig 8) Monochrome LCD sounder/plotter
A typical monochrome (black and white) sounder display. Monochrome are still the most common type of display, particularly in the lower price market, but are being overtaken by colour LCD displays.

The system used to display the echoes is the most obvious difference between sounders. Today two main systems dominate today's market, monochrome liquid crystal displays (LCDs) and colour liquid crystal displays. Monochrome LCDs (Fig 8) are by far the most common and are still the preferred choice of most operators, however colour LCD screens are fast overtaking the monochrome units, creating an increasingly growing niche, particularly in the upper performance range, and upper price range, of sounders. All LCD types use a screen that is made up of pixels. Pixels is short for picture elements and refers to the tiny 'dots' which make up the display (Fig 9), the same as on a domestic television receiver. Obviously the more pixels the finer will be the picture and the greater will be resolution, or ability of the sounder to display fine details. LCD sounders (Fig 6) have many advantages over the paper-graph machines that they replaced. The LCD screens are flat and comparatively thin, which allows designers to produce small, compact sounders. The displays are easy to see in bright light, even direct sunlight, and backlighting on modern LCDs has improved to such a degree that night viewing is now also first class.

Using membrane type, press-button controls there is no necessity to open the case during normal operations—in fact many sounders cases are welded together at manufacture and cannot be opened, even for service—unlike the paper sounders which had to be opened at regular intervals to replace the graph paper. It is now possible to manufacture totally sealed units that are truly waterproof, a boon for most small boat operations.

Due to the inherent reliability of modern electronic components and the machine manufacture of the printed circuit boards used in sounders, as well as strict testing and quality control, two year warranties are, almost without exception, standard for all modern sounders. Today's sounders offer a degree of reliability undreamed of only a few years ago.

Monochrome LCD displays are generally black and white or blue and white although other colours are possible.

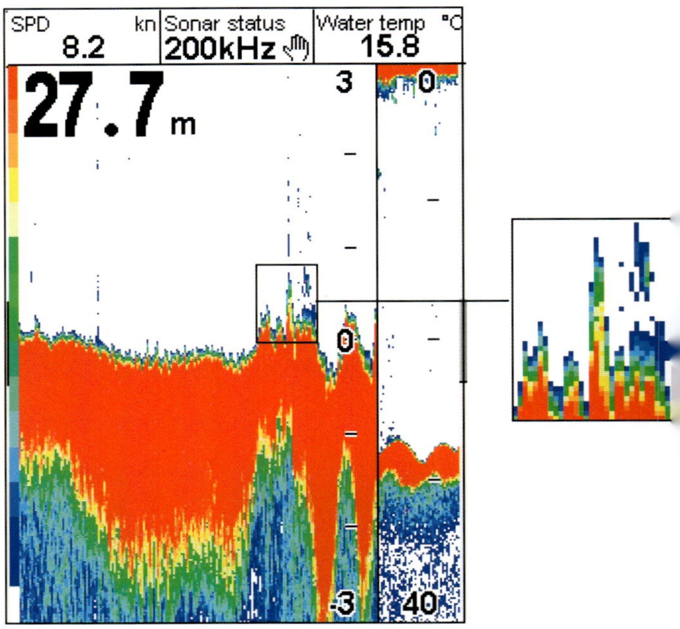

(Fig 9) Pixels
LCD and video displays are made up of small elements called pixels. Pixels are turned on and off to make up the picture. In monochrome sets the activated pixels are either black or in a shade of grey. On colour sets the pixel will be coloured depending on the strength of the returning echo. If there is no signal the pixel remains dormant and is not visible. The small section of the display in the illustration has been enlarged to show individual pixels, which make up the image.

Chapter three
Transducers

The transducer has been described as the 'Heart' of a sounder system, and justifiably so. If you think of a transducer as a speaker and microphone built into one housing it makes the principal of how it works easier to understand. A speaker converts electrical signals into sound signals in the same way the transducer converts the output pulses from the sounder into sound pulses. These sound pulses travel through the water as small pressure waves. When one of these waves strikes an object in the water, such as a fish or the bottom, part of the wave bounces back, this reflected wave is known as the returning echo.

When the returning echo wave strikes the transducer, it acts as a microphone, converting the sound wave back into an electrical signal. The transducer receives the echo in the interval between each transmit pulse. The transducer is in the receiving mode for about 99 per cent of the time and only transmitting for about 1 per cent of the time. All of this happens in a very short period of time, a few microseconds in fact, and the repetition rate of the sounder pulses is high. (Fig 10)

The analogy of throwing a pebble into a still pond will help to visualise the sound patterns produced by a transducer in transmit mode. When the pebble is thrown into the pond, small waves or ripples radiate from where the pebble hits the water surface. The waves spread out from the centre, that is, they move out in concentric circles. When the transducer transmits its output pulse it is directed downward below the boat and these pulses also spread out in concentric circles, downward and outward, as they make their way into the deeper water. These waves actually spread out in a cone shape, making what is known as the transducers 'cone angle'.

Cone Angle

The angle at which the output pulse is transmitted varies between transducers depending on their intended applications, ranging from a narrow angle of around 8 degrees to a wide angle of about 50 degrees. The various cone angles is one of the parameters that affects sounders' performance in various depths. Manufacturers change the cone angles of transducers by varying the diameter of the transmitting element—the piezoceramic crystal. The larger the element the smaller and more concentrated the beam, the smaller the element, the wider and less concentrated the beam.

(Fig 10)
Cross-section of typical transducer housing
A transducer is made up of several parts, the piezoceramic crystal, which may also be called the piezoceramic element, the housing, the acoustic window, encapsulating material and sound absorbing material. All of the various components are fitted into the housing that supports and protects them from damage in the rather harsh environment in which it will be used. The piezoceramic crystal is the heart of the transducer. The crystal vibrates and produces sound waves when excited by the transmitter pulse from the sounder. When an echo returns to the transducer the pressure of the sound waves cause the piezoceramic element to vibrate and this vibration produces minute electrical currents that are processed by the sounder and then displayed on the screen. The acoustic window is the face of the transducer through which the sound waves travel and is situated between the piezoceramic element and the water. Sound absorbing material surrounds the piezoceramic element, except in the window area, and is used to damp out any unwanted pulses and echoes. The whole of the transducer's elements and the electrical connections and cable are encapsulated and sealed in the housing.

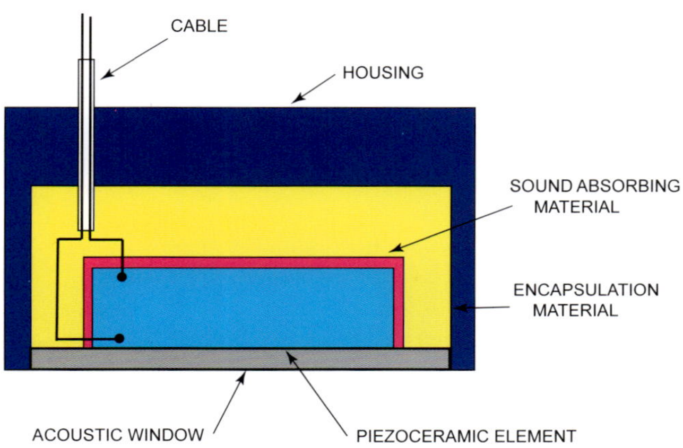

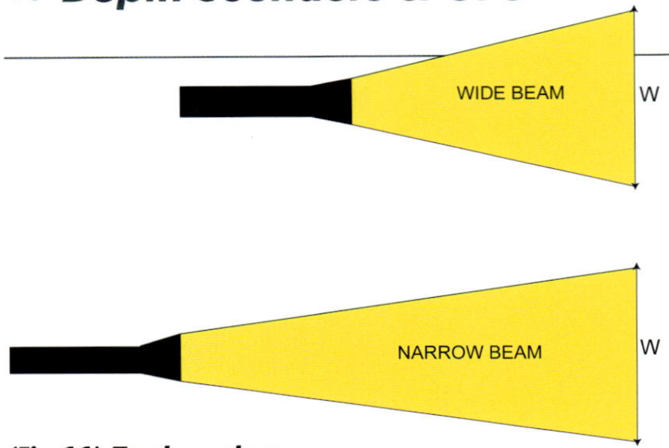

(Fig 11) Torch analogy

The concept of wide and narrow beam transducer cone angles can be likened to a torch beam. The wide beam torch produces a large circle of light at a comparatively short distance, whereas the narrow beam torch needs to be much further away to illuminate the same area. This analogy can be applied to transducers beam angles.

To fully understand transducer beam angles an analogy of a flashlight beam makes the concept easier to grasp. (Fig 11) Imagine for a moment that you have a torch with an adjustable beam. When you have the wide beam selected the light will cover a large area enabling you to see details over this area, however the strength of the light will drop off quickly and not penetrate very far into the darkness. If a narrow beam is selected the light is concentrated into a smaller beam that will travel out into the dark a lot further, but will only illuminate a small area up close. This simple example can be easily transposed to sounder transducer beam angles. Wide beam angles cover large areas but the energy is dispersed quickly and, when used in deeper water, only weak echoes will be received. Narrow beams cover smaller areas but penetrate deeper water much better. This analogy does not take into account the frequency of the transducer and the effect it has over depth penetration of the sounder.

Transducer beam angles (also called cone angles), are precisely like a torch beam, the sonic energy spreads out from the transducer in a cone shaped pattern. (Fig 12)

The drawing used to illustrate these principals is somewhat over-simplified for the purpose of clarity. Firstly, the sound cone is drawn as a clear, clean cut line, which is not strictly true. Going back to our torch example, from experience you know the light beam from a torch is not clear cut, the light intensity fades off towards the edges of the light beam, until it reaches a point where there is insufficient illumination to be of any use. This is just like the sound beam from a transducer. As the sound spreads out from the centre of the beam it reaches a point were there is insufficient energy left to be of practical use. This point is usually where the signal has fallen to half strength, usually expressed as -3dB (decibels). However, if, for simplicity's sake, you think of the beam as being clear cut, it is easier to understand, and for all practical purposes this is how a transducer sound pulse appears to behave.

Closely related to cone angles, a question that is often asked is what is the area covered, (or 'seen') by a transducer at various depths? The diameter covered by the transducer beam with a 20 degree cone angle may be calculated by using a rough rule-of-thumb. It states that the transducer will cover a circular area with a diameter approximately one third of the depth.
For those with a mathematical bent the following formula may be used to calculate the diameter of the circle covered by a transducer.
Diameter of beam = 2 x depth x tangent
(½ cone angle)

For example, the diameter of the coverage of a 20 degree cone angle transducer in a 5 metre depth would be:

(2 x 5) x tangent(20/2 degrees)

This is 10 x 0.17632 = 1.76 metres.

Our rule-of-thumb says the diameter will be 5/3 or 1.66 metres. Close enough for most cases.

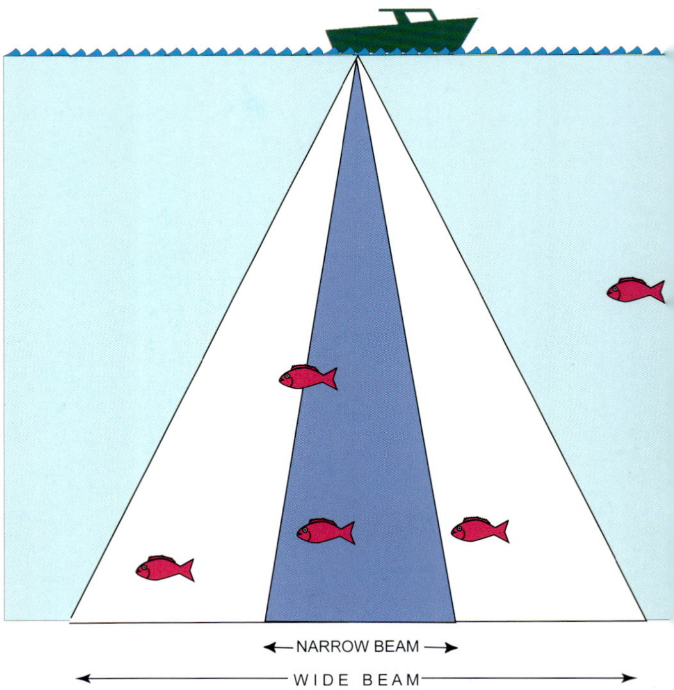

(Fig 12) Wide and narrow cone angles

Transferring the torch analogy to transducers, the output is focused into a beam that is directed downwards and, depending on its design, the beam is wide angled covering a large area or narrow covering a smaller area. While he wide beam will 'see' more landscape, a narrow beam shows more detail. However, many other factors will influence the choice of transducer.

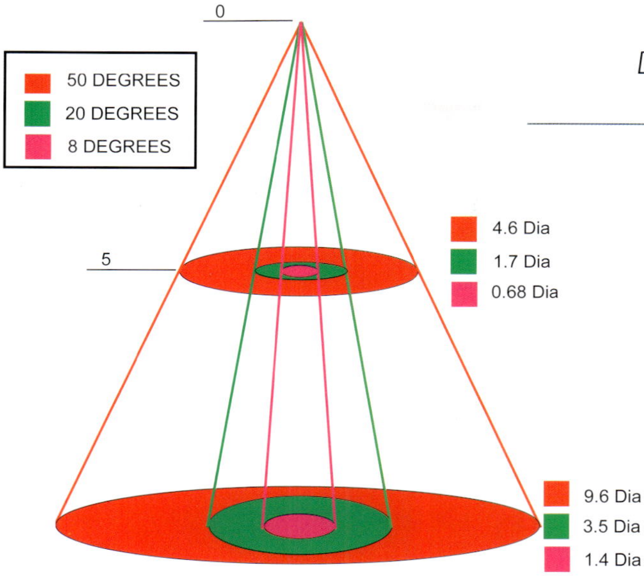

(Fig 13) Areas covered by transducer's beams
An important aspect of transducer cone angles is the actual area on the bottom that is covered by the beam—the transducers 'footprint'. This illustration has been drawn to scale to help visualise the effects of different cone angles. The outer edges of the transducer beam are determined when the sound intensity has fall to half power (-3dB) when compared to the centre of the beam. This is the industry standard but some manufacturers may quote the outer edge of their transducers at -6dB, which is a quarter of the sound intensity. The method used to determine the beam angle is usually quoted in the transducer's specifications.
The dimension on the illustration is quoted in dimensionless units, to enable easy conversion to any system either feet, metres or fathoms.

The figure (Fig 13) is a graphic representation of three popular cone angles. This has been drawn to scale to give a true representation of the difference between cone angles. Also note units have been used to allow for easy conversion to any measuring system, metres, feet or fathoms.

However, this depends on how the cone angle is measured. The industry standard is when the sound level from the centre of the cone falls below -3dB, that is, half the sound strength, this point is considered to be the outer edge of the beam. But some manufacturers of recreational sounders measure the cut-off point of the beam at -6dB, one quarter of the sound intensity, giving the impression the transducer has a much wider cone angle. It is therefore important to know which system is being used to describe a transducer's performance.

The American company Airmar has been responsible for many breakthroughs and innovations and make a huge range of transducer for just about any application. So comprehensive is their range that today almost all sounders on the recreational market, regardless of their country of origin, use transducers manufactured by Airmar. Two of the major advances in transducer design has been the dual beam (cone angle) transducer contained in a single housing and dual frequency transducers also in a single housing. (Fig 14)

(Fig 14)
Transom mount transducer
An example of a typical Airmar duel frequency, transom mounted transducer.

A few years ago most sounders were supplied with 'ual beam 200 kHz transducer, generally a broad beam of 20 degrees and a narrow beam of eight to eleven degrees. The cone angle was switched from a menu on the display. The current trend among manufacturers seems to be to supply dual frequency transducers, usually 200 kHz and 50 kHz frequencies. The 50 kHz frequency is inherently made as a wide cone angle of typically 50 degrees and the 200 kHz element is a narrow beam. This combination offers a great degree of versatility that will be explained detail in the operation chapters of the book.

Side imaging is a new method of displaying bottom features that uses an entirely different technique, which is full explained later under the heading Understanding Side Imaging. It uses a special transducer, which is illustrated (Fig 15) mounted with a standard transducer.

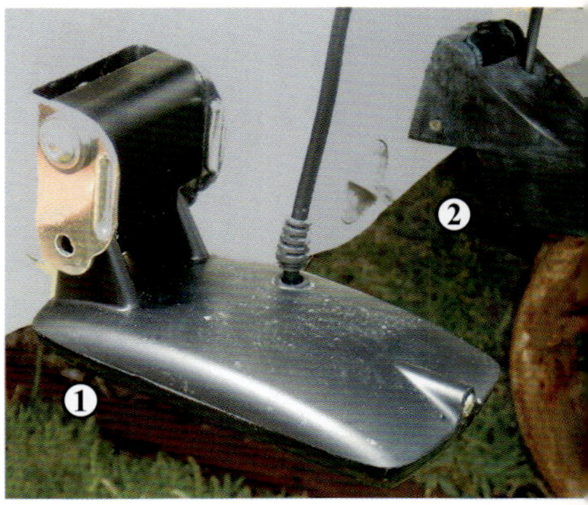

(Fig 15)
Transom mounted transducers
Two transducers—a side scan (1) and 'standard' 50/200 kHz frequency unit (2)—mounted on an aluminium cat. Due to the narrow transoms on these types of boats, each transducer was mounted on separate side of the transom. This boat is used extensively for testing and evaluation of electronic equipment and has four transom mounted transducers, two on each hull.

Frequency

An important parameter of transducer performance is frequency, which determines maximum operational depth and definition. A high frequency transducer transmits shorter pulses more frequently than lower frequency units. Referring to the 'pebble in the pool' analogy used earlier; a small pebble will produce small waves that do not travel far on the pool's surface. These smaller waves on striking a small obstacle will bounce back. It is the same with high frequency sound waves, they are more sensitive to small objects and the returning echo will show crisp, highly detailed images on the display screen. However, the high frequency sound wave will be absorbed more quickly by the water. The common high frequency transducers operates at 200 kilohertz (kHz) and have a practical depth limitation under good conditions of about 180 metres (600 ft).

Referring again to our analogy, if a large rock is thrown into the pool, large waves will be created, much further apart than the waves made by the pebble, in other words these large waves will be at a lower frequency. These big waves will wash right over small objects with little or no reflected wave. Applying this thinking to transducers, lower frequencies will travel down to greater depths but do not 'see' small objects and do not produce as pictures as crisp and sharp as the higher frequencies.

Another way of understanding frequency is by wavelength that is the distance from one wave crest to next. At 200 kHz the wavelength is approximately 7.4 mm (0.29 inches) and a 50 kHz transducer produces wavelengths of approximately 29 mm (1.15 inches). It follows that the 200 kHz transducer would 'see' a fish around 7 mm long, whereas the 50 kHz would only detect a fish over 29 mm. (Fig 16)

However there is another factor that comes into the equation, and that is how an echo sounder actually sees a fish. The greater part of any echo returning from a fish comes from the air bladder. Almost all fish have an air bladder that allows them to adjust their buoyancy for the depth. Some species have large air bladders in proportion to their size and these fish give stronger, darker echoes than others with relatively small bladders.

It is the gas in the air bladder that is considerably different in density to the flesh and bones of the fish and that of the surrounding water. The difference in density is what the sounder 'sees'. It is also this 'air bladder' phenomena that helps to give different fish species a characteristic echo, which helps in the identification of fish images on the screen.

Keeping this in mind and remembering how lower frequencies need larger targets to be able to detect them, the actual minimum size in practice is greater than theory suggests.

Output Power

Output power, sometimes called transmitted power is the amount of energy used to generate the sonic pulse and is measured in watts. Values as low as 100 watts can be used in simple sounders designed for shallow water use or up to a 1000 watts for large, deep water sounders. Unfortunately the output power is specified in one of two systems, RMS units (root mean squared) or peak-to-peak power, which leads to quite a deal of confusion. Both systems are expressed in watts, but for the same output power the peak-to-peak reading is about eight times greater than that quoted in RMS. That is, if a sounder's output is specified at 100 watts RMS, it could also be rated at 800 watts using the peak-to-peak system.

Transducer Housings

Another transducer variation is the housing that contains the piezoceramic element. Most sounders sold to the recreational market come complete with a transom mount transducer, suitable for transom mounting on outboard powered craft. There are however, a number of other types of housing available to suit other types of mounting, the 'puck' type for gluing to the inside skin of fibreglass boats, through-hull-mounting for installing the transducer transmitting through the boat's hull. These types and their application will be discussed in detail in the chapters on installation.

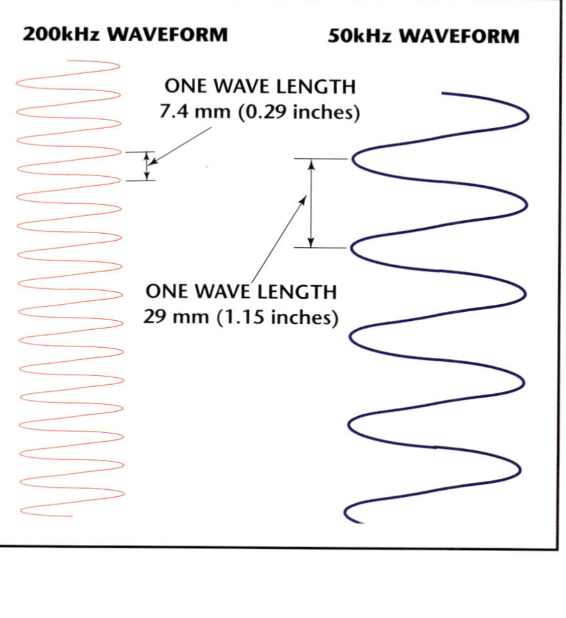

(Fig 16)
Comparison of 50 and 200 kHz waveforms
Comparison of waveforms for 50 kHz and 200 kHz frequencies. Another way of understanding frequencies is with wavelengths, which is the distance between the wave crests. Since the wavelength of 200 kHz is much shorter than 50 kHz, 7.4 mm (0.29 inches) to 29 mm (1.15 inches), the higher frequency can resolve targets that are close together and display them as single echoes much better than the lower 50 kHz frequency.

Chapter four

Primary Controls

This chapter describes the primary controls of sounders, in this context primary refers to the basic controls to be found on just about all sounders. This chapter describes these features and how to use them. However, before describing the practical side of operating a sounder, here are a few words on how the sounder's outgoing pulse and returning echoes are processed and displayed on the screen. Many operators have problems visualising how the display on the screen is created and tend to look at it as if it were a snapshot, which is not quite correct. Study closely the illustration (Fig 17) which should help you to understand the concept.

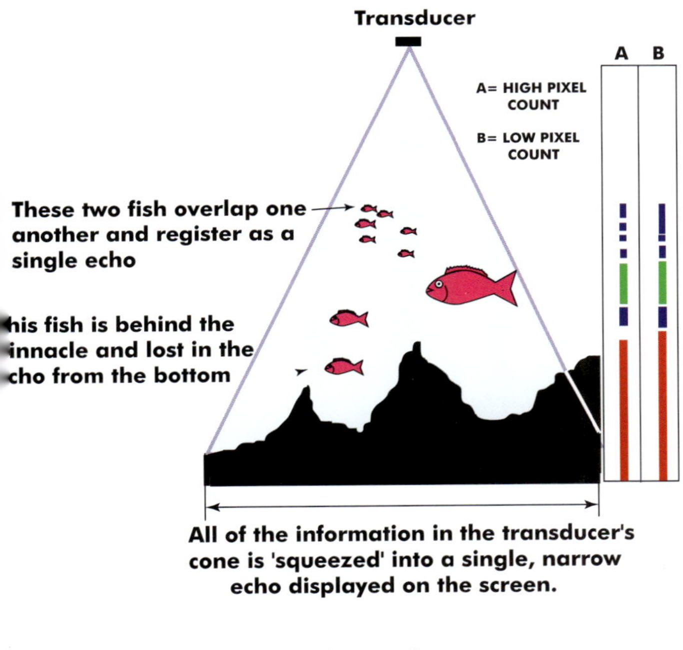

(Fig 17) Single transducer pulse
The diagram represents a single transducer pulse displayed on the sounder screen. The two graphs, 'A' and 'B' represent a single vertical row of pixels on the extreme right of the screen. 'A' represents a high pixel count and 'B' is a low pixel count. Note, the baitfishes that are close together are shown as a single trace, whereas the high pixel count separates into separate traces. The different strength of the echoes is distinguished by separate colours. The colour palette is typical of that used by 16 colour palette sounders, dark red at the top of the scale is the strongest colour and dark blue is the weakest echo, clear (no colour) is the absence of any signal and that pixel is turned off.

A sounder display is made up of echo returns from single sound pulses, thousands of these pulses are needed to make up a single display screen on the sounder. As each set of returns from the pulses is displayed the sounder picture moves slightly to the left, adding the most recent pulse to the screen's right hand edge and dropping the oldest pulse from the left side of the screen, thus a total picture is built up. This may be easier to understand if one imagines the old paper graph sounders. A stylus would move down the paper 'printing' the echoes and the paper would then move ever so slightly to the right and the next pass of the stylus would then print on the paper alongside the previous stylus printout, building up the familiar paper graph. This is exactly the process on the LCD screen, except the whole process is electronic.

Now since the pulse from the transducer is in the form of a cone, one must imagine all the returns from the pulse are 'squeezed' together laterally to form a single thin echo that is displayed on the screen. In the illustration this single return is displayed at the right of the screen, two examples of the echo are displayed, the 'A' display is of a high pixel count (fine detail) and 'B' of a low pixel count display. Notice how the small fish echoes tend to be clumped together with a low pixel count. The single pulse display is very like that of an A-scope display described later in detail. The smaller fish are displayed in blue, larger fish as green and the bottom is shown as red. Study the illustration and you will notice because of the squeezing effect, a fish echo has been 'hidden' by the bottom display.

This concept is important and if you can visualise how the display is constructed, it makes understanding what the sounder is showing you, so very much easier.

Today, even the most basic echo sounder is a highly sophisticated item of electronic equipment and it would be a shame if the operators did not fully utilise these capabilities by not taking the time or effort to understand its operation. This chapter will show you how to access your sounders features and how, and why, to adjust them to achieve optimum performance. Time spent learning how to get the best from your sounder will be handsomely repaid in better soundings and hopefully, better fishing.

It would be impossible to describe the actual mechanics of accessing the various controls on each and every brand and model of sounder; operators should refer to the instruction book for their particular model for the sequence to actually access the functions.

All sounders have the same basic controls, except in the very basic models, while some also have features and functions unique to their particular brand or model. With the power of microprocessors ever increasing, today's sounders possess a huge range of options, many of these functions are really 'gilding the lily' and are novelty features rather than practical applications. However features, which may appear to be frivolous to some operators, are hailed as very worthwhile innovations by others.

Almost without exception the operating parameters and features of modern sounders are accessed by the use of menus (Fig 18). Before microprocessors were used to manage sounder functions, the choice of features was limited to perhaps half a dozen or so. Microprocessors opened a whole new world of dozens of functions that could be added to even economy model sounders at little, if any, additional cost. These additional features led to a proliferation of press-buttons on the unit's keyboard and, unless the user had a photographic memory, it was impossible to remember all of the strokes needed to operate the sounder's added features. So to make the operation of these units practical they were supplied with waterproof 'how-to' sheets that were carried in the boat as a reminder for the operators of how to access the functions. The menu system, borrowed from computer technology, came into being and today all units use this simple system. Menu technology has meant sounder keyboards today have fewer keys than ever before but control a greater range of functions than ever before.

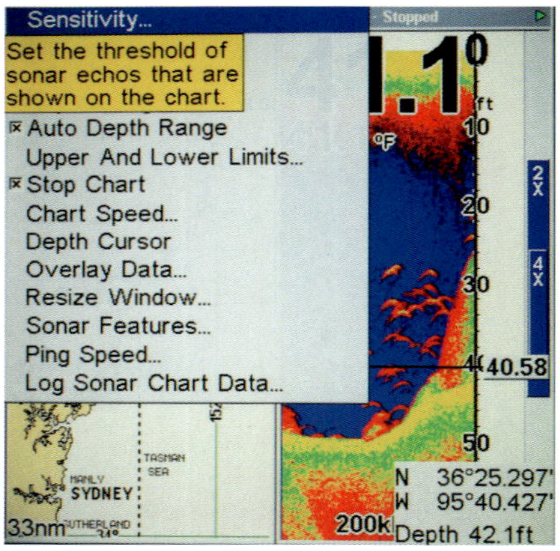

(Fig 18) Menus
The illustration is of one of the menu screens from a Lowrance LMS 525 sounder. The sensitivity item has been selected on the menu and a help screen is displayed to instruct the operator as to what the selected function is. This help screen is optional. Also selected is the 'stop chart' function. Since the illustration is an actual photograph of the screen, the screen image was frozen to reduce the possibility of movement in the picture. The menu may be made partially transparent to enable the operator to see the display underneath the menu.

Compare the illustration of modern sounder keyboards to that of Lowrance's X15 paper graph sounder (Fig 4) and (Fig 19).

Three basic sounder functions have the greatest effect on the display and the ability of the operator to interpret the information displayed on the screen. These are sensitivity, range and frequency. While frequency is usually just a matter of swapping between two choices, sensitivity and range are adjustable through large ranges and it is these two functions that have the greatest bearing on sounder performance.

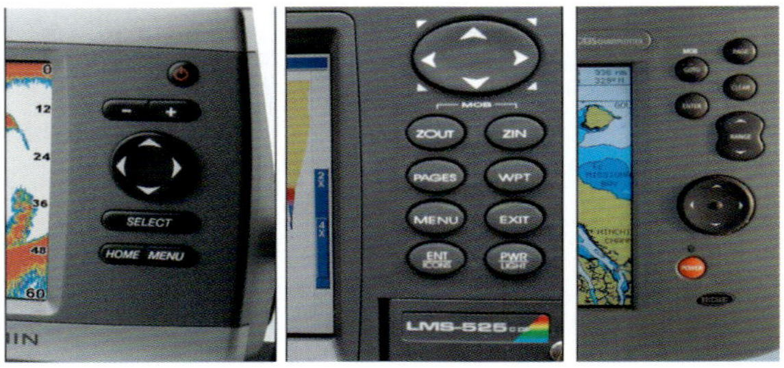

(Fig 19) Keyboards
Three keyboards, from left to right, Garman, Lowrance and Raymarine illustrating the simplicity of modern sounder's keyboards. Compare these boards with those of the Lowrance X-15, a much more complex board but with far fewer features

Sensitivity

Sensitivity may be called gain on your unit, but both terms mean exactly the same, they describe the level at which the sounder's receiver is operating. The time honoured simile of a sounder's sensitivity being likened to the volume control on a car radio is a good one. As you drive further away from the radio station, you need to turn up the volume to keep the same level of sound for comfortable listening. (Fig 20)

It is the same with the sensitivity control on your sounder, as the water depth increases you must turn up the control. Also, the correct amount of sensitivity is required if the sounder is to be able to display weaker echoes coming from small targets such as small (bait) fish. Even more, the correct amount of sensitivity is necessary to properly discriminate between hard and soft bottoms, such as sand and rock. To take the radio receiver example further, when you adjust the sensitivity on the sounder you do not change the unit's output power, this always remains at maximum—just the same as when you change the volume on the radio, you do not alter the broadcast station's output power. (Fig 21)

When using a sounder in impoundments, lakes or rivers it would be unlikely one would ever need full gain to obtain quality soundings because of the depth of water. However there are situations when having a reserve of sensitivity is very useful, these situations will be explained shortly, but first a word about adjusting sensitivity and Auto settings.

(Fig 20) above

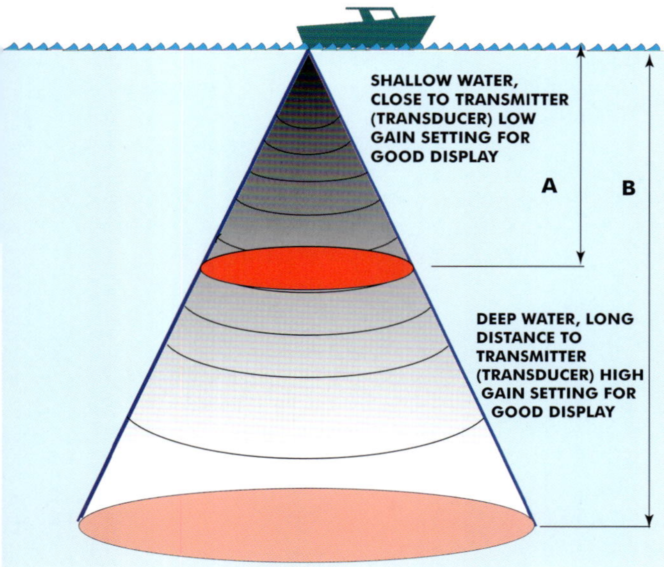

(Fig 21) left

There is a widely accepted rule that says that you should manually adjust the sensitivity to increase the gain until 'clutter' appears on the screen and then back-off the control until only a small amount of clutter is left. In other words, always run the sounder with the maximum amount of sensitivity consistent with the amount of noise you can accept. Follow this golden rule to obtain optimum performance from any sounder. Clutter, sometimes called noise, is interference that appears all over the screen as small dots. If too much clutter is present then those very important, fine details in the sounding will be obscured. Refer to (Fig 22), which is a black and white sounding showing a classic example of clutter. This is a sounder image of a wreck in a saltwater lake. Note that the clutter shows both above and below the bottom, indicating it is true clutter and not small particles in the water.

(Fig 22) Clutter : below

The sounder image was taken in deep water (100 metres). Because of the depth and the small size of the baitfish schools, maximum gain was employed which created a fair degree of clutter on the screen. Referring to the car radio analogy once again, when the volume is turned up high there is always some background noise present, this is exactly the same with this sounding, except the noise is visible, similar to 'snow' on a TV screen, when the signal is weak. Although the clutter is present, it was not so heavy as to obscure the baitfish schooled above the bottom.

(Fig 20) & (Fig 21) Radio analogy : above

Sounder sensitivity can be likened to the radio in a car. When the car is close to the radio transmitter, ('A') the signal is strong and the radio only needs a low volume setting to give a level of sound for comfortable listening. When the car is some distance away, ('B') the volume needs to be increased to near maximum to give the same level of sound.

Remember when you change the volume on the radio you do not alter the broadcast station's output power, it always remains the same. It is the same with a sounder, changing the sensitivity does not change the output power, this always remains at maximum, it only changes the receiver's sensitivity. The second diagram transposes the analogy to a sounder. In shallow water the bottom is close to the transducer (transmitter) 'A' and the sensitivity required for a good image would be relatively low. In deeper water, the distance from the transducer (transmitter) 'B' is much greater and lots more sensitivity is needed for a usable image.

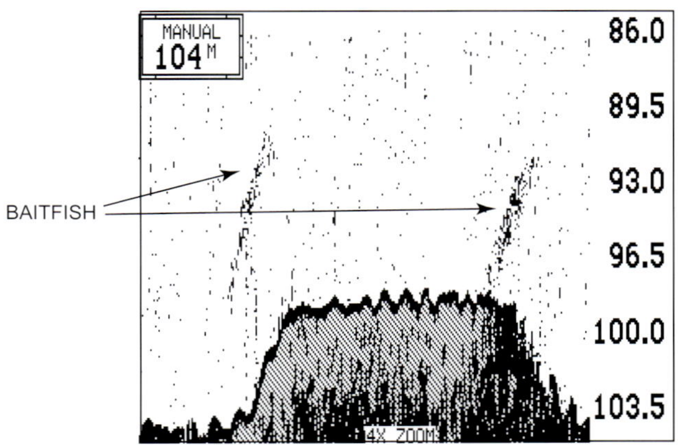

Modern sounders, almost without exception, have auto gain control. This auto feature does work reasonably well in most cases, however if the operator puts in the effort and learns how to adjust the sensitivity manually for differing situations the pictures obtained will give a great deal more detail. Auto sensitivity tends to always set the gain on the low side, this gives a good clean looking picture with little or no noise, but you may be missing important detail such as fish and bottom texture. (Fig 23)

Another trap users can fall into is one of familiarity. When fishing one particular spot regularly, you get to know the setting on the sensitivity control and tend to automatically set the control at this position. However, the amount of the sound signal the water absorbs varies considerably from day to day, the sensitivity setting that was spot on today may not be the best setting for tomorrow. Some of the factors that effect the transmission of a sound signal through water are suspended matter in the water column, organic matter such as dirt or mud, animal and vegetable matter such as plankton and even the temperature of the water can have a discernible effect. Any of these factors can change from day to day—even from hour to hour—which demands constant attention to the gain control to achieve the best possible results.

An example of the difference water conditions can have on sound transmission was the case when I fished the edge of the continental shelf. At a depth of approximately 180 metres (600 feet) the bottom quickly shelved down to about 700 metres. Using a Lowrance X15 paper graph sounder and a narrow cone angle transducer (8 degrees) operating at 200 kHz, I received a solid bottom sounding at the edge of the shelf and maintained a sounding for some distance over the edge, which was exceptional depth readings for this type of sounder.

Two weeks later I was sounding some distance inshore of the shelf on a favourite fishing spot in 100 metres (330 feet) using an identical sounder set-up. Normally at this location a sensitivity setting of 75 per cent gave solid, clean images, but on this occasion I had to use maximum sensitivity to obtain a usable sounding, which even then was not very good, the image was almost obscured by heavy clutter. The sea conditions on both days were excellent and the water, on the surface, was a deep, clear blue. The only difference was that there had been a period of about four days of rough weather a week before. Obviously the water had been stirred up by the heavy seas, resulting in a large quantity of sediment that was absorbing the sounder's pulses.

The moral is never take for granted what the water conditions will be and always adjust the sensitivity to suit the actual conditions. Many anglers may feel this is just too much fiddling about; however the attention to small details is usually what separates the top fishermen from the mediocre, and correct adjustment of the sounders sensitivity can make that difference.

(Fig 23) Sensitivity

These three sounder screens exemplify the marked effect sensitivity has on soundings. All three soundings were made by running the boat over the same snag at the same speed. The snag was a sunken tree on top of a rise in the bottom. Similar dead trees on the dam edges showed many small, fine branches. The screen on the left marked 'Excessive Sensitivity' depicts the tree as an extension of the bottom, the fine branches appear to be solid and every particle in the water, including tiny fish and plankton, is showing strongly. These echoes are so strong that they are masking larger fish.
The second image marked 'Insufficient Sensitivity' only shows the main larger branches of the tree as a fairly weak echo—refer to the colour palette on the left of the sounder screens—and there is no strength in the bottom display.
The last screen 'Correct Sensitivity' has enough sensitivity to show the main trunk of the tree as a strong (red) echo and the small branches as nice 'firm' display. The surrounding water is clear of clutter but there is sufficient sensitivity to show up small concentrations of baitfish to the left and above the tree and a single larger fish in mid water.

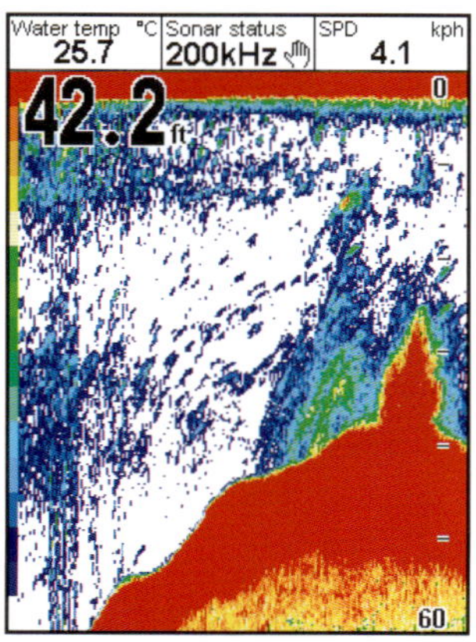

EXCESSIVE SENSITIVITY

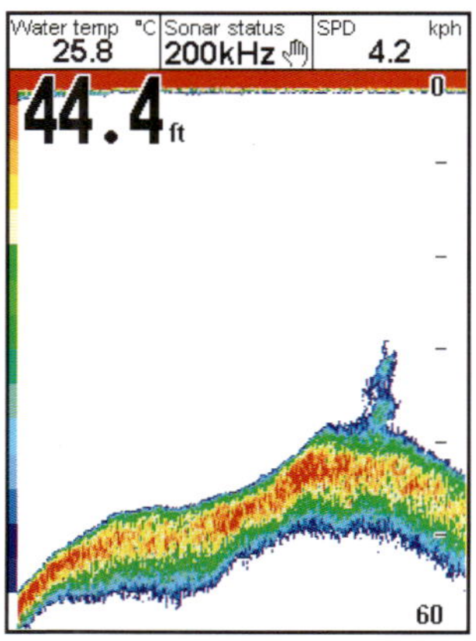

INSUFFICIENT SENSITIVITY

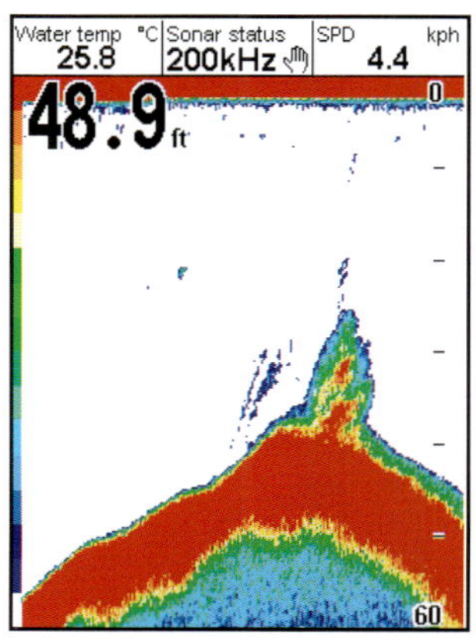

CORRECT SENSITIVITY

Exceptions to the rule

There are occasions when, to achieve special results, the 'Golden Rule' is ignored, although only to a small degree. The occasions are when you are looking to find very small baitfish or plankton concentrations, or the position of thermoclines. It is then an advantage to have higher sensitivity settings than normal, there will of course be more clutter on the screen but by careful observation, backed by experience, you will be able to identify the baitfish. (Fig 24)

The advent of Digital Signal Processing (DSP) has somewhat changed the part sensitivity plays in displaying the underwater scene. For a full description of this new system see the chapter on recent innovations, but the returning echo is processed by the digital processor that adjusts the sounder's parameters to produce the best possible display, and this includes sensitivity. The sensitivity is adjusted across the whole of the sounding many thousands of times in each pulse. For example, take the sounding of a baitfish school over a wreck. The DSP is in effect altering the sensitivity of the bottom echo to give a strong solid echo, but reducing the sensitivity of the echo of the baitfish schools to allow the separation of individuals in the school.

DSP is still a relatively new sounder feature and operators will take some time to fully explore all of the nuances of the system to find how best to exploit the remarkable features of this major advancement. (Fig 25)

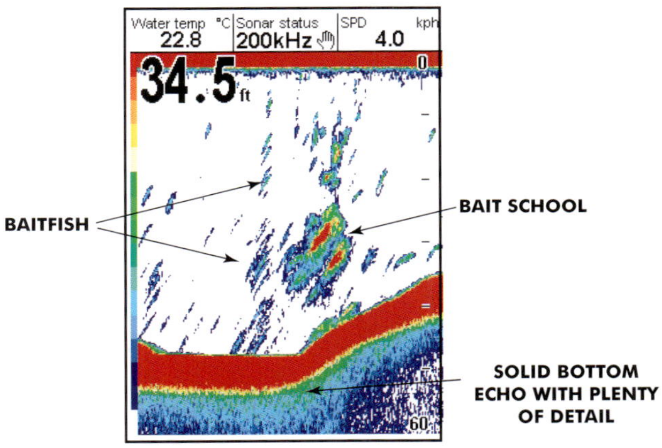

(Fig 24) Sensitivity and baitfish

The sensitivity on this display of a sounder screen is correct for the conditions. We were looking for baitfish concentrations and were using a comparatively high setting. The baitfish are all moving upwards in the water and the bait school we were looking for was quite dense—indicated by the red centre of the school. The bottom display is solid with plenty of detail. There is also a good showing of late scatter below the bottom trace. The densely packed baitfish school tended to indicate predators were probably harassing them. We were unable to raise a fish despite trying every lure we had in the boat—that's fishing!

(Fig 25) Digital Signal Processing

A screen download to illustrate the definition and clarity offered by this new concept. A 115 gram (4 oz) sinker and a prawn bait dropping into a school of fish in 63 metres (206 feet) of water. The boat had been anchored and was slowly (0.4 knots) coming up tight on the anchor. (1) The boat is just coming over a school of fish hanging just off the bottom. The bait and sinker (3) is descending from the surface and as the bait closes onto the school (2) individual fish can be seen as they move up out of the school to investigate. A few seconds after this download was recorded the angler hooked up and landed a sergeant baker, a local fish not esteemed for its eating qualities.

The gaps in the trace of the bait and sinker (4) are caused by the rolling motion of the boat swinging the transducer beam from side to side. Also, the trace is not recorded until the sinker and bait have dropped down far enough in the water column to come into the transducer's beam. A frequency of 200 kHz was selected to give the best resolution, however this transducer has a relatively narrow beam angle, which accentuates the movement of transducer beam.

(6) The sinker and prawn bait similar to that depicted in the soundings. This sounding illustrates the high definition possible with the Digital Signal Processing not only showing the path of the sinker and bait, but also clearly discriminating between the school of fish and the bottom trace (5).

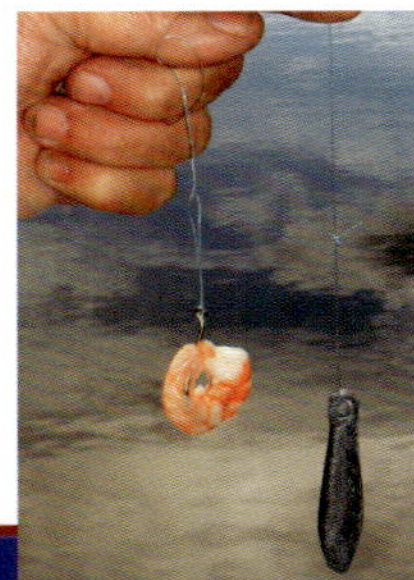

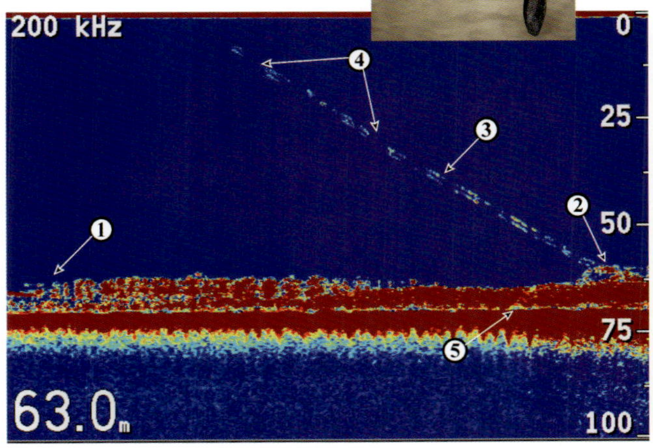

Range, Shift and Zoom

The functions of range, shift and zoom are all closely related and refer to the section of the underwater picture the operator wishes to view.

In the following examples, ranges and depths are fairly large and one would be unlikely to use settings of this magnitude in impoundments or estuaries. A number of dams do have water that is at least this deep and even greater, but generally the ranges and depth setting used would not be as great, but by using larger figures to illustrate the principals of shift and zoom, the theory is easier to visualise. (Fig 26)

Range is the setting that determines the depth scale or rang the sounder is displaying. In earlier models this was usually limited to half a dozen settings e.g. 0–30, 0–60, 0–120, etc metres and sometimes phased ranges, e.g. 0–30, 30–60, 60–120, etc metres. However modern sounders are microprocessor controlled, making the choice of range much greater, usually increasing by 10 unit steps. These units could be feet, metres or fathoms, but for ease of illustration we will assume the readings to be in metres.

Range settings are the basic depth controls of a sounder, but except in shallow depths they have a major drawback. To illustrate this problem imagine a sounder operating in 20 metres of water with the range set to 0–30 metres, when the boat runs over a small school of fish in the water column which are about five metres thick and are about five metres above the bottom. On a screen 75 mm high, which is about average, the school would cover an area of about 5 mm—not large but plenty big enough to be easily noticed. Now take the same scenario but increase the depth to about 80 metres, with the depth scale set on 90 metres, the same school of fish that displayed about 5 mm would now only show as just over a millimetre, difficult to see among the normal bottom clutter.

To overcome this problem, designers use either zoom or shift, which fundamentally do the same job in different ways. Zoom is generally a fixed percentage magnification of the bottom section of the picture. This simply means the operator can magnify the bottom by a fixed factor such as 2 times, 4 times or 8 times. So in our illustration of 90 metre range setting, by zooming 4 times the picture would display the bottom from 67.5 metres down to 90 metres, a zoomed picture of 22.5 metres, almost identical to our sounding using the 30 metre range in 20 metres depth.

Shift setting allows the operator to manually select the section of the water column to be displayed, again using our example the range setting would be left on 30 metres and then 'shifted' down to read from 60 to 90 metres. Using either the zoom or shift control has given the same result, it allows the fisherman to view a 30 metre section of the water column including the bottom. In offshore waters, a 30 metre band is a very convenient section to view. If a greater magnification is used, the wave action will become so prominent on the bottom trace as to obscure details. Wave action is rarely a problem in lakes or dams and a smaller band than 30 metres may be used, however there are other factors to be considered when selecting what will be your ideal range setting.

One of advantages of selecting a fixed band is that targets are always the same relative size on the screen, regardless of the water depth. This means you can quickly relate to sizes displayed on the screen to their true size, and this is particularly true when it comes to recognising and identifying fish echoes. Some models of sounders use the system of setting the viewing band by nominating the upper limit and the lower limit, which is another way of shifting the display.

There is another element to be considered when deciding on the range to use and this is the underwater terrain that you will be fishing over. If there is considerable depth variation, such as commonly occurs in dams constructed in rugged country, then a relatively narrow band will entail a lot of range changing if you are using manual or a great deal of changing in the 'Auto' shift mode. This brings us the subject of 'Auto shift' or 'Auto Zoom'.

Auto shift and zoom is available on most of today's units and its operation is much smoother than earlier models, but I strongly recommend using manual control of these features. When in auto mode the internal processor is constantly looking to keep the picture in the bottom third of the screen by locking onto returned bottom echoes. However if a bubble or other disturbance returns an echo that is above the bottom the processor recognises this as the bottom and locks onto it, changing the display to suit the 'new' bottom. Once this false echo is lost, the unit then must go looking for another bottom echo. This constant flicking from one range to another can give a greatly distorted picture that is difficult to interpret. This is particularly so when the boat is travelling at any appreciable speed or in choppy conditions. By 'locking' the unit into manual these problems can be minimised.

I find a 20 metre band is a very practical band to use in most dams but it is something of a personal decision as to which range suits your needs best. If you fish in natural lakes you will find the variations are not so great and nor does the depth change so rapidly. In these circumstances a narrower band may be practical although using very narrow bands can lead to a 'cluttered' display due to tiny fish and particles forming echoes that are disproportionately large.

As is true for just about every rule there are exceptions. There are times when it is desirable to view the whole of the water column—from the surface to the bottom—such as when trying to locate thermoclines or when searching for schools of fish in mid water. Also, when surveying an area for the first time it is advantageous to be able to see on one display the entire water column. This gives a more realistic view of the make-up of the underwater scene than would a view of segments or bands, which would present a disjointed overall picture. See also split screens displays.

There are occasions when a large magnification may be desired to define small targets such as tiny bait, both fish and crustaceans (it is quite possible to see and identify prawns or shrimp at high magnifications) or even smaller plankton.

Scroll Speed or Chart Speed

Scroll speed is the rate at which the display advances across the screen. This speed may also be called chart speed, which is a hangover from the early days when sounders used a roll of paper to record and display the soundings. The speed does have a significant effect on the appearance of the display, a fast speed 'stretches' out the displayed picture, which can be useful when looking for small targets such as baitfish or fish down very close to the bottom. The disadvantage is there is what is known as a short history. This means the display is only on the screen for a relatively short period of time.

Slow scroll rates provide long histories, which can be helpful when comparing data, such as bottom details, which were recorded some time ago. The drawback of slow rates is that small details tend to be compressed and can be difficult to distinguish from the surroundings.

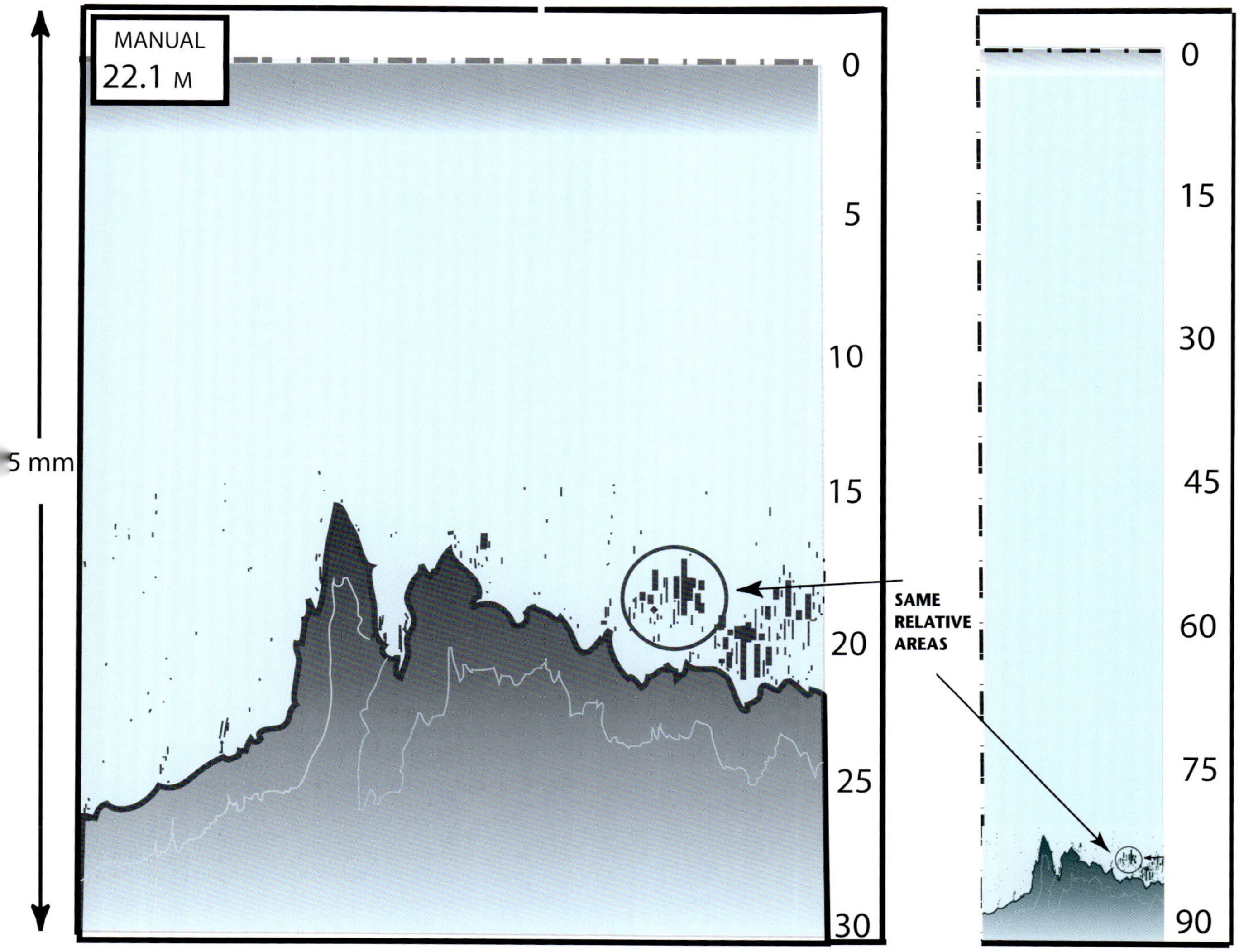

(Fig 26)
Compression of details by increased range
These images illustrate the effect depth range has on the apparent size of fish images. The right hand image has a range or band of 30 metres and the school of fish covers an area of about 5 metres and are 5 meters above the bottom. Assuming the sounder screen to be 75 mm tall, the image of the fish would be 5 mm high. The right hand image represents the same school of fish but now in a depth of 90 metres. The fish image would now be only about one millimetre, quite difficult to see and recognise.

Chapter five

Secondary Controls

Secondary controls are those features that are not used as often as primary controls and may not be common to all models or brands of sounders.

Frequency

As mentioned earlier, changing frequency is a straightforward function that is usually accessed from the operating menu or via a dedicated press button, check the operation manual for details of your particular model. While changing frequency is a simple function when and how, to use this feature is another story.

Single Frequency Transducers

To the average recreational sounder user or those who are in the process of looking around for a new unit, the technical discussion of sound and frequencies may be interesting, but they simply want to know—what can the various transducers do for me and what is the best to buy? Before any meaningful answer can be given, it must be determined just what are the conditions the sounder will be expected to operate in.

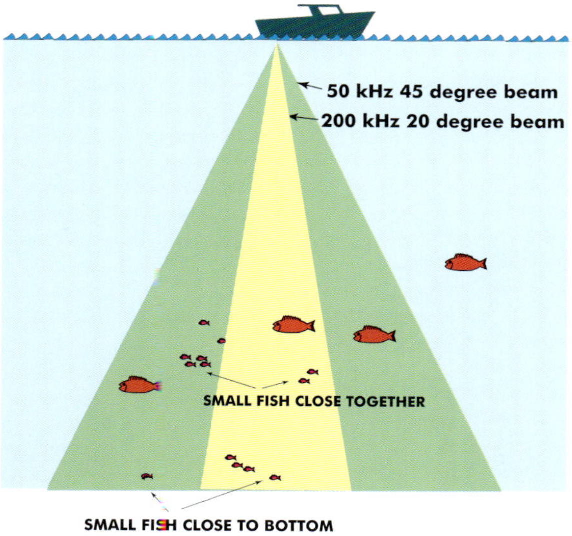

(Fig 27) Definition of 50 kHz and 200 kHz frequencies
Comparison of wide beam 50 kHz transducer and narrow beam 200 kHz transducer. The number of small fish in the 50 kHz transducer beam will probably be shown as a single echo and the small fish close to the bottom will become part of the bottom echo. The small fish in the 200 kHz transducer beam will be separated into separate images on the screen

For the majority of applications, 200 kHz will provide good, useable soundings and if your choice is limited to a single frequency transducer, then a wide angle 20 degrees and 200 kHz transducer is the preferred choice for shallow water work. At a pinch, it will give acceptable pictures in water depths of up to 100 metres, depending to a large degree, on the power output of the sounder and the cone angle of the transducer.

With few exceptions, all sounders on today's market will be supplied as standard with a dual frequency transducer, however there are still some sounders with only single frequency transducers and for these units the wide (20 degree) transducer is still the best compromise.

Dual Frequency Transducers

If a choice is available of a dual frequency then this is definitely the best option, even if only comparatively shallow water sounding is envisaged. Dual frequency transducers are invariably 200 and 50 kHz, and most times the 200 kHz transducer will be a narrow cone angle, anything from 8 degrees through to 12 degrees, while the 50 kHz will probably be a 45 degree cone angle. As mention earlier, the 50 kHz sound pulses travel through water with less loss of power than higher frequencies, enabling good soundings to be obtained in deep water with lower gain, or sensitivity, settings, but 50 kHz cannot generate soundings with as good definition as 200 kHz can. Definition is the ability of the sounder to define or separate small targets such as baitfish and is usually referring to separation in a vertical direction. If you look at the illustration, there are a number of small baitfish depicted as being close together in the left hand side of the 50 kHz beam. Because of the poorer definition of the low frequency transducer, these small baitfish will be clumped together on the display screen as one large image and would probably be mistaken for an echo of the larger fish nearby in the water column. Similarly, the small fish near the bottom will blend into the bottom echo and be virtually invisible.

Now look at the illustration of the 200 kHz, 20 degree beam. The baitfish would be separated and appear as separate images on the screen and could not be confused with the single large fish. Also the small fish close to the bottom would be shown as a separate echo. (Fig 27)

There is another factor to be taken into consideration when discussing definition and that is the pixel count of the display. There is little point in having a transducer capable of producing an echo that is capable of discriminating between fish only 50 mm apart when the sounder screen has too few pixels to be able to display the two, closely spaced targets as separate images.

With all of these disadvantages, one would be excused for asking why use a 50 kHz frequency at all, the simple answer is the 50 kHz will acquire soundings in deep water where a high frequency and higher definition transducer could not produce a useable picture. Any sounding is better than none at all and in these conditions, the shortcomings of the frequency are easily overlooked.

The wide angle of 50 kHz transducers also has other advantages—when searching for a small target such as a wreck or small pinnacle, the wide beam covers a much greater area of the bottom, called a footprint. For example at 30 metres a 200 kHz, 11 degree beam has a footprint of about 95 square metres, while the 50 kHz is almost 500 square metres. If you are trolling off a downrigger, in either salt or fresh water, the wide beam enables you to view the downrigger bomb and see fish approaching and even taking the lure. The illustration of 'comparison of beam angles and frequencies' explains the relationship in a graphic form.

While the foregoing may have given the idea that low frequency soundings are useless for seeing fish and identifying the species, this is certainly not the case. Some years ago I had several trips on a commercial drop line boat to commission a large colour video sounder and train the crew in its use. Because of the depths the boat was to work in, a 28 kHz transducer was selected. The area fished was on the canyons with depth ranging from 800 to 1000 metres (2,600 to 3,280 feet). The catch varied, including several deep water species of cod known as hapuka and blue eye trevalla, as well as a large number of small sharks called green eyes, averaging about two metres in length. By the second day I was able to recognise fish laying down the sides of the canyon and accurately nominate them as either green eyed sharks or fish species.

Since 50 kHz frequency offers wide angle sounding, dual frequency transducers usually feature a narrow beam 200 kHz element. Having a narrow beam angle, 200 kHz transducer has several advantages. The narrow beam with a small footprint makes finding accurate boat positions much easier, also the narrow beam will penetrate deep water better because of the concentrating of sounder output power into a smaller area.

While all of above discussion on the wide angle transducers, still hold good, another relatively new system, side imaging, has brought a new dimension to wide angle transducers, particularly when searching for bottom features. For more details see the section on side scanning.

The phenomena of double or second echoes, while common to all frequencies, it is more pronounced when using 50 kHz transducers. Second echoes occur when the pulse of sound waves fired from the transducer strikes the bottom and are reflected upwards towards the surface, some of these reflected sound waves—the 'echo'—are received by the transducer, processed and displayed to provide the sounding. However, much of the echo also strikes the surface where, because of the great difference in density between the air and water, these sound waves are reflected back towards the bottom. When these reflected sound waves strike the bottom they are again reflected upwards and may be detected by the transducer and displayed as a bottom echo. However because they have made the journey from the surface to the bottom twice they will be displayed at double the depth and as a much weaker image because of the extra distance they have travelled in the water and because of reflected losses. A second echo will not be displayed unless the sounder range is such that the true bottom will be shown in the top half of the screen. (Fig 28)

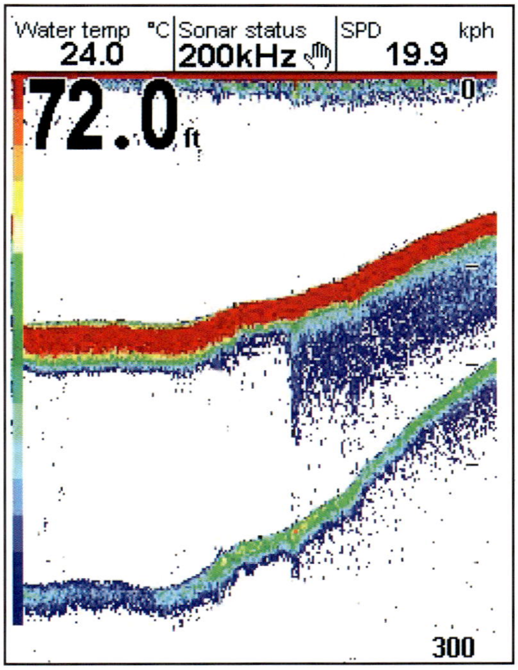

(Fig 28) Second echo

A second echo, or second bottom, is formed when the echo from the bottom strikes the water surface and is reflected back towards the bottom. This reflection takes place because of the vast difference in density between water and air. When the reflected sound wave strikes the bottom it is again reflected towards the surface—and the transducer—and is registered as another bottom trace. While second echoes occur in all soundings they are only visible on the display if the original bottom trace, the first echo, is in the upper half of the screen, otherwise even though the second echo is there it is below the actual display. Second echoes are much stronger when the bottom is hard, such as gravel and rock.

Transducer technology has made quantum leaps forward even in the last decade. It is not all that long ago when on purchasing a sounder it came with its own transducer and that was it, no choice. If a 50 kHz transducer was needed for deep water work you had to purchase a completely separate sounder unit. Today, even a modest sounder is very likely to have at least a two frequency transducer, perhaps even three frequencies, as well as different beam angles. The versatility these multi-frequency transducers offer the serious angle is truly amazing, but you must learn how to use them if you are to reap the benefits they offer. If you are out on the water and the fishing is slow, turn on the sounder and have a play. Change frequencies and see what the effect is on the screen, adjust the gain on the different frequencies and note the effect, not only on the bottom trace but also on any baitfish that may be around.

To reiterate, the most common frequencies found in modern sounders are 200 kHz and 50 kHz, but 455, 120, 83, and 28 kHz are all used. The fundamental principle is the lower the frequency the better the depth penetration and the higher the frequency the better the definition. Of course, this means that no matter what frequency is chosen, it is going to be something of a compromise.

If the sounder is designed simply for shallow water work, then the highest practical frequency will be used—that is 455 kHz. Humminbird, amongst other manufacturers, makes several models using this frequency, dual frequency sets using both 455 and 200 kHz. as well as the 957CV which uses 455, 83 and 200 kHz. These low frequency, high definition units are targeted at freshwater users, particularly those who fish in shallow lakes where depth penetration in not a problem. Nevertheless, the vast majority of sounders use 200 kHz which has proved to be the best all round compromise between good definition and reasonable depth penetration. This is particularly so if only one frequency is fitted.

Once you get the feel for using the various transducer frequencies, swapping between frequencies will become second nature and your catch should certainly improve.

Frequency, range zoom and sensitivity are the most important features of any sounder, however there are a number of other functions that greatly enhance the performance of modern sounders.

Alarms

Alarms are to be found on just about all sounders and, when used intelligently, they can be assets—however they do have the potential to drive one mad at times. Alarms are generally divided into two basic types—bottom alarms and fish alarms—although some units may divide the fish alarm into a third division know as a zone alarm. Low battery voltage alarms are also available if the sounder is fitted with a battery monitoring feature.

Fish alarms are, as the name suggests, simply an alarm that activates whenever an echo that the sounder determines to be a fish echo is detected. The part of the sentence in italics is the key to the successful operation of this facility on your sounder and is also, at the same time, the weak point of the whole system. Obviously the sounder has no intelligence as such, and can only determine if a particular echo is created by a fish by having the echo meet certain criteria contained in the unit's software. While the software in today's sounders, even the more basic units, is incredibly sophisticated, certainly when compared to units of only a few years ago, it can still be fooled by signals that, to a human observer, are certainly not fish.

This problem of the identification of spurious objects as fish is what can be so frustrating about fish alarms. The alarm signal is generally quite strident as they need to be to be heard over engine and water noises. But when the sounder is constantly 'sounding off' because it is seeing all sorts of things in the water—such as bubbles, silt, surface clutter, weed etc—which it perceives to be fish, the sound becomes quite annoying and most operators, particularly new users, tend to turn this feature off and never bother with it again. This is a shame because when one understands the limitations of the system and works around them, fish alarms can be a powerful tool in the armoury of the modern electronic fisherman.

FISH ALARM

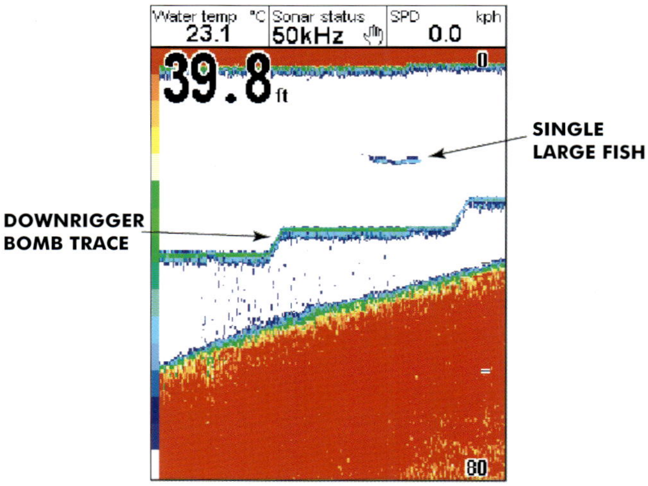

(Fig 29) Fish alarms

While this illustration is not strictly of a fish alarm, it does show a situation in which an alarm could have been used and proved to be helpful. The downrigger is set at about 30 feet (9 metres) and set to troll 10 feet or so above the bottom. As the bottom shallowed, the downrigger bomb is adjusted to maintain the separation above the bottom. The single large echo was not noticed until the boat was past its location. Had the fish alarm been positioned to monitor the water column above the downrigger bomb the anglers would have been alerted and could have raised the bomb into the strike zone.

To many fishermen, the main appeal of having a fish alarm is so they can run along at speed with the alarm on and find schools of fish. Unfortunately this is just what you cannot do, except in ideal conditions. The boat, when travelling at speed, creates lots of spurious echoes, mainly bubbles, which the sounder identifies as fish and sounds the alarm. The fish alarm really comes into its own when the boat is at anchor or drifting in reasonably clean water.

Take the scenario of slow trolling in reasonably calm water. The sounder's range is set to display a reasonable band of water above the bottom and the fish alarm is activated. Should the boat drift over a school of fish or even a few large fish, off goes the alarm, drawing the fishermen's attention to their presence. This is particularly useful when using a downrigger, fish can be located that may be above or below the downrigger bomb's depth, which can then be adjusted to get it into the strike zone. Of course, the observant angler should be watching the sounder's screen all the time, but the fish alarm is a convenient backup.

One point to keep in mind is that the transducer's cone angle should be selected so that the downrigger bomb is not in the sounder's view, otherwise the alarm will continue to sound. Another alternative, particularly when the downrigger is operated near the bottom, is to set the fish alarm just above the bomb. (Fig 29) The advantage of this method is the downrigger bomb is visible on the sounder screen.

A factor to be taken into consideration with fish alarms is the sensitivity setting, if this is too high every little particle in the water column will be displayed and the alarm will be singing away almost constantly. By judicious adjustment of the sensitivity control, only targets of a reasonably large size will be displayed and the alarm will reflect a truer picture of what is happening below the boat.

The bottom alarm is perhaps more straightforward. The alarm is set at a pre-predetermined range that will trip the audio alarm signal if the depth becomes greater or less than the set range. Take the case of looking for a pinnacle that you know rises from a bottom of say 10 metres deep up to a depth of 7 metres. The bottom alarm is set to sound when the bottom becomes less than 9 metres and this takes the task of constantly checking the sounder away from the skipper who can concentrate on running the boat.

This alarm can also be used as an anchor watch, particularly at night when a dragging anchor may not be noticed. If you have anchored in 10 metres of water, set the alarm range for 8 to 12 metres and if the boat drifts into deeper or shallower water the alarm sounds. While this is a very useful method of keeping anchor watch, a GPS is even better, but if you don't have a unit, then the sounder is a valuable asset.

A zone alarm is basically the reverse of the bottom alarm, the bottom alarm activates when the bottom becomes deeper or shallower than the setting, a zone alarm trips when an echo is detected within the set range. While zone alarms can be useful in detecting fish in certain depth ranges their application is somewhat more specialised than the fish and bottom alarms, and is not used all that much.

Alarm facilities are available on even the most basic of sounders but are used very little by the average angler, yet with a little thought they can be one of the most effective attributes of any sounder.

Surface Clutter Control

Another feature seldom used is surface Clarity Control (SCC), which is sometimes also called Variable Time Gain (VTG), which is used to reduce surface clutter. Surface clutter is the noise displayed on the screen that extends down from the zero line at the top of the screen, representing the area just below the water's surface. Surface clutter is caused by a number of factors—aeration from wave action, plankton, temperature inversions causing layering of the surface water and silt etc floating on or near the surface.

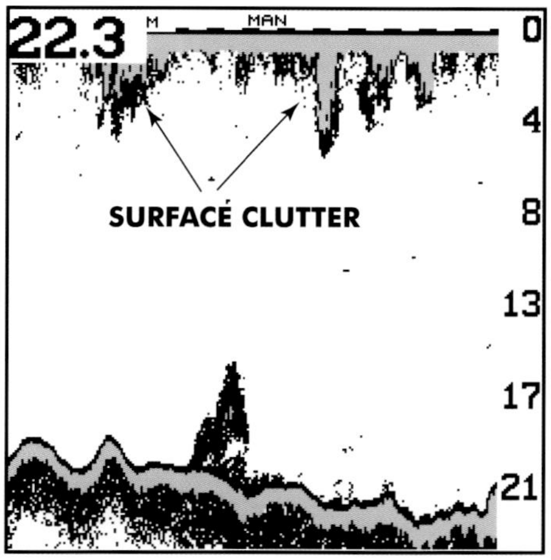

(Fig 30) Surface clutter
This sounding illustrates the surface clutter phenomena. Surface clutter is noise or interference, which extends down from the surface into the water column, which may be caused by small bubbles, plankton, silt etc on, or just under, the surface. In this case the sounding was made on the down current side of a shallow reef. There was a heavy swell with a lot of broken and stirred up water on the reef that was being swept by the current into the area where the sounding was made—which accounts for the uneven nature of the surface clutter. (The big swells can be identified from the 'ups and downs' reflected in the bottom trace). Although the surface clutter extended down six metres at times, it did not cause any problems as the main interest was in bottom fish bait schools.

Surface clutter can extend down from the surface to several meters, sometimes even more, and obscure details in this zone. Obviously this type of clutter only becomes a problem in shallow water, although I recall an occasion in early spring when there was a particularly strong plankton upsurge, which was extending down to almost ten metres, but this is exceptional. Usually two to three metres is the most you will ever encounter.

Since the particles that cause surface clutter are going to be quite close to the transducer, they are exposed to the strongest section of the transducer's output pulse and will return a very powerful echo, way out of proportion to their size. This means it does not take a lot of material in the surface layer to give a strong return on the display. (Fig 30)

Surface clutter control overcomes this problem by reducing sensitivity of the first part of the returning echo, the actual degree of signal reduction is controlled by the operator and usually varies from so slight it is hardly noticeable to quite powerful. When using SCC it must be remembered that this function actually reduces the sensitivity in the surface zone, so any fish in the surface zone, particularly small fish, will also have their return echoes reduced. Correct use of SCC is something of a balancing act—just enough cutting of the signal strength to reduce the surface clutter so that fish can be spotted close up to the surface, but not too much to obliterate the fish echoes.

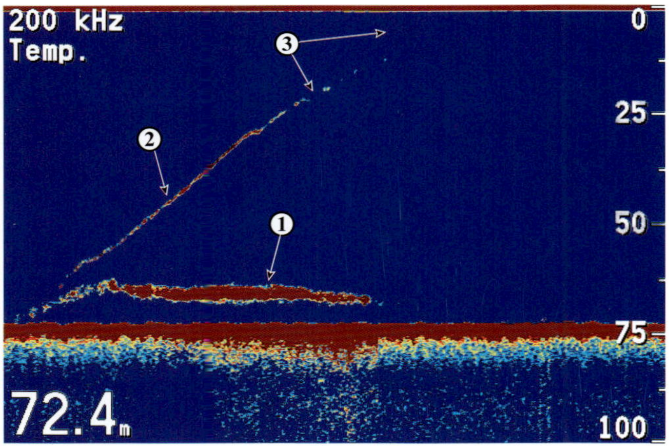

(Fig 31)
Clean' sounding with digital processing
This download is the reverse of Fig 25, in that it shows a hooked fish, a nannygai, (2), being lifted from the school and retrieved up to the boat. The nannygai are a baitfish for snapper in the deeper water and while they are a bait stealing pest, often a good snapper will be hooked in and around the school. (1) Is a small school of nannygai, hanging well above a relatively featureless bottom. (3) Shows the broken trace caused by moving transducer beam as explained in Fig 25.

While the call for SCC is not great, when the sounder is used in the relatively shallow waters of estuaries, lakes etc SCC can become a very worthwhile attribute. Take the case of an impoundment after heavy rain. Quite often the run-off will be slightly less dense than the main body of water and will float on the surface. The fresh water usually contains lots of silt and other sediments and these form a dense surface clutter. Another case is water at different temperatures often form into layers that are know as thermoclines. Thermoclines are important fish indicators, but they can also form narrow layers on or near the surface.

All of these scenarios are what surface clutter controls were designed for and they really come into their own in these conditions. If you strike a sounding that is showing a lot of surface clutter, have a play with your SCC and discover its potential. The recent introduction of digital processing of the returning sounder echo, mainly by adjusting the signal bandwidth, has eliminated surface clutter problems. (Fig 31) See the section on this technology for full details.

Split Screen

A split screen facility allows the operator to divide the display screen into two separate displays. The screen is generally split vertically but some models also provide for dividing the screen horizontally. The division of the screen is also adjustable allowing for the operator to have a larger percentage of the screen for the most important display and a small section for the less important feature.

With a split screen one screen can display two separate frequencies or zoomed and standard display etc. Take the case of the angler searching the bottom for a small feature or baitfish close to the bottom using a zoom view to present an enlarged view of the bottom. But the angler still wishes to see the whole of the water column in case there are baitfish, thermoclines or other details well above the bottom—a split screen is the answer. (Fig 32)

It is also possible to split the screen into 200 kHz and 50 kHz display. A practical instance of this would be if the operator was using the wide angle view of the 50 kHz transducer to search for a bottom feature, e.g. wreck or pinnacle, but was also using the higher definition of the 200 kHz frequency to check the presence of bait or other small details.
Features such as bottom lock and A-scope would not be practical without split screens. (Refer to 'Bottom Lock' and "A-scope").

Bottom Lock

Bottom lock is another sounder description that can be ambiguous. It can refer to two different sounder features depending on how manufacturers view this feature. Originally the term bottom lock referred to the sounding mode that displayed the bottom as a straight line, regardless of any changes in the bottom depth or features. The rationale for this being that the magnification of the bottom display in the normal sounding mode is limited by wave motion causing the boat to rise and fall, thus increasing and decreasing the distance (depth) of the bottom. (Fig 33) See the illustration to better understand this phenomenon. In the example illustrated the swell is reflected on the bottom 'creating hills and hollows' of two metres. While this distortion is acceptable in a display covering 20 metres, (See the section on range and zoom) it would be intolerable if the display was reduced to only three metres, but this magnification is often desirable if looking for fish close to the bottom or trying to identify small fish. Note that even though fish may be some distance off the bottom they still appear on the sounder display as if they are moving up and down with the swell.

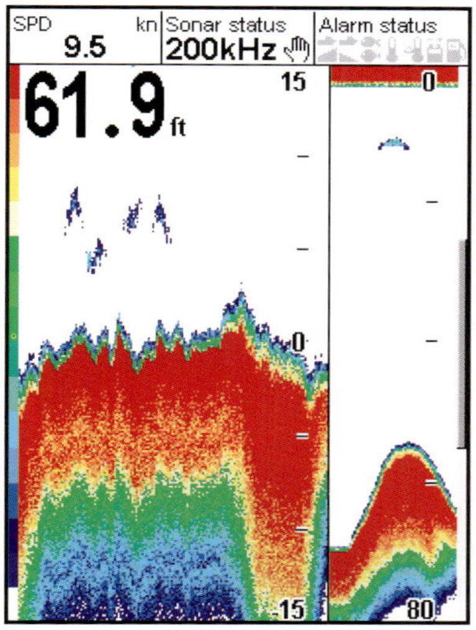

(Fig 32) Split screens

Since the centre of interest for this sounding was the top of a reef pinnacle, the Navman Fish 4500 was set up in the split screen mode with the larger (two thirds) part of the screen showing a zoomed range of 30 feet (9 metres). However, there had been some large yellowtail kingfish caught in this vicinity so we also wanted to keep an eye on the whole water column and had set the smaller split from the surface to 80 feet (24 metres).

Notice the zoomed screen shows lots more details than the surface to bottom view, including a couple of substantial pods of bait, however on the un-zoomed display shows a single large fish close to the surface—bingo, it was a king-fish. We anchored on this reef and after some solid berleying we caught several good fish on live baits floated under bal-loons. Had we been only viewing a zoomed screen we would have missed the fish high in the water.

ILLUSTRATION OF A BOAT SOUNDING IN A TWO METRE SWELL. THE DIFFERENCE BETWEEN DISTANCE 'A', WHEN THE BOAT WAS IN THE TROUGH AND DISTANCE 'B' WHEN THE BOAT WAS ON THE CREST OF THE SWELL IS TWO METRES

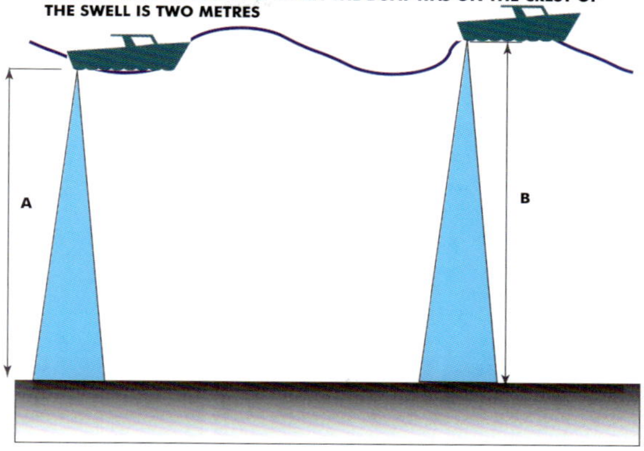

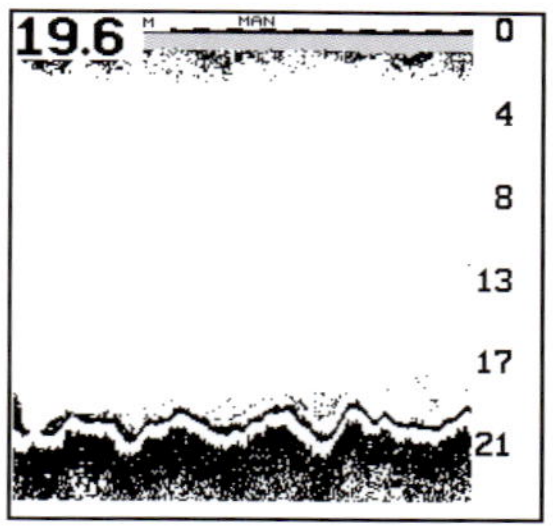

ACTUAL SOUNDING OF A FLAT BOTTOM MADE IN A TWO METRE SWELL. THE SURFACE TRACE IS SHOWN AS A STRAIGHT LINE BUT THE SWELL MOTION IS 'REFLECTED' IN THE BOTTOM SOUNDING GIVING THE IMPRESSION THE BOTTOM IS 'HILL AND HOLLOWS'. NOTICE THE SMALL BAITFISH CLOSE TO THE BOTTOM THAT APPEAR TO BE FOLLOWING THE UPS AND DOWNS OF THE BOTTOM.

(Fig 33) Wave motion

The upper illustration represents a boat sounding in a two metre swell. The difference between point A when the boat is in the wave trough and B when the boat is on the crest is two metres, the size of the swell. In effect, as the swell passes under the boat the actual distance to the bottom, the depth, increases and decreases.

The lower illustration is an actual sounding made over a flat bottom in a two metre swell. The bottom echo accurately reflects the 'up and down' motion of the boat, but the surface trace is a straight line. The small fish down close to the bottom appear to be following the up and downs of the bottom, but this is only an illusion.

Bottom lock overcomes this problem by 'straightening out' the bottom trace so that it always appears as a straight line no matter how large is the sea or the swell. However, this 'straightening' also removes any features of the bottom, such as holes or reefs etc, making a standalone bottom lock display almost meaningless. To be of any practical use a bottom lock display must be accompanied by a split screen displaying a 'normal' view. Using a split screen in this mode it is possible to relate the rather graphic bottom lock display to the normal sounding showing bottom features. (Fig 34)

Bottom lock is a somewhat difficult display to interpret, but for those operators who have persevered and mastered it the rewards are well worth the effort, particularly in locating and identifying fish species that spend a lot of time close to the bottom and do not congregate in dense schools.

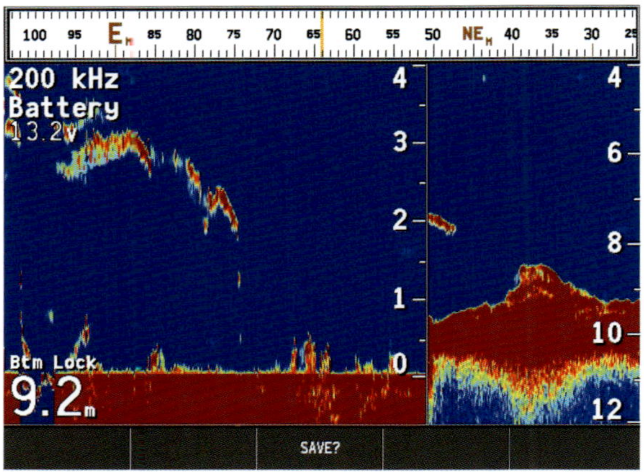

(Fig 34) Bottom lock

This screen download shows the standard screen display on the right and the bottom lock view on the left. Notice on the bottom lock display the depth scale reads from the bottom upwards, in this case from zero to four metres.
The standard sounding shows a bump on the bottom, which is reasonably hard as indicated by the late scatter, but the standard type sounding does not clearly show whether the soft areas (yellowish colouring) on the top of the rise are tightly packed bait or part of the bottom structure. However, the bottom lock display shows the bottom is in fact solid with some small overhangs, probably a small area of solid bottom. Had baitfish been present they would have been displayed above the straight line of the bottom. The echoes standing up from the bottom are from a vertical, spindly type weed that grows on any hard bottom in the lake.

A-Scope

Another powerful split screen combination is Standard/A-Scope. A-Scope is another method of displaying the echoes returning to the transducer. The strongest echoes are shown as brownish-red colours and extend out to the right side of the screen and being the strongest echoes extend the greatest distance from the left side of the display. Weaker echoes are shown as shades of blue and the bar extends for a relatively short distance. (Fig 35)
To many operators, A-Scope is a mystery consisting of a jumble of different coloured bars and lines that are constantly changing, and are seldom, if ever used. However, with a little bit of time and patience spent to gain an understanding of A-Scope a whole new method of interpreting sounder information is opened to the operator.

The section on colour pallets mentions that each of the colour steps is separated into 1.5 dB steps, however if the signal strength varies by less than 1.5 dB then the standard display 'rounds off' the difference in strength showing the echo as a single colour. With the A-Scope type of display, not only does the sounder display the colour, but the length of the bar also provides a subtle indication of the comparative signal strength.

The A-Scope is an instant display of the sounding beneath the transducer at that instant and constantly changes as the boat moves over the bottom and the sounder updates the display. There is no 'history' as in the standard display and the screen must be observed constantly to evaluate what the sounder is seeing at the moment. This characteristic of A-Scope virtually demands that a standard screen display be used in a split screen configuration if one is to have an idea of the bottom profile. While the constantly moving bottom band will indicate if water depth is increasing or decreasing, the standard screen is needed to really see the bottom profile. The main purpose of A Scope is to identify fish, particularly small fish close to the bottom or otherwise obscured amongst bottom structure. A-Scope is also useful when there are large, dense schools of baitfish, which may tend to hide large fish.

Another plus for A-Scope is identifying hard and soft bottoms. Hard rock or gravelly bottoms produce lots of late scatter, which is evident below the true bottom trace as longish strokes, usually in shades of blue. (Fig 35a) Late scatter is very evident on the A-Scope display. Because of A-Scope's transient nature, reducing the scroll rate of the standard display tends to render the A-Scope display a little easier to interpret.

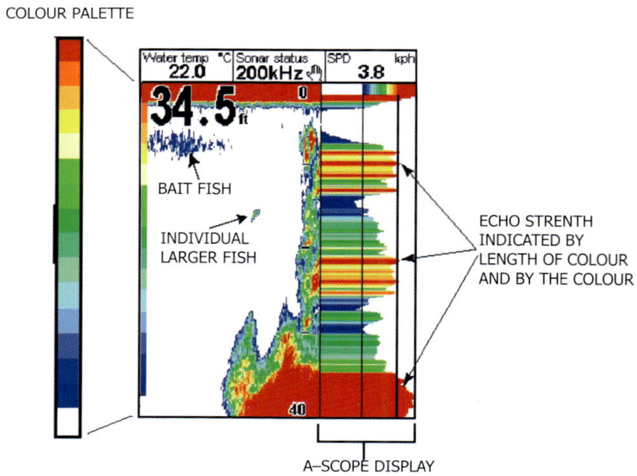

(Fig 35) A-Scope

A-Scope is a representation of the sounding in real time—it show what is happening at this instant in time and there is no history of previous soundings. the history is retained in the standard view (left side of the screen). The strength of the echoes is presented on the screen in two ways, by the length of the colour bars and the colour of the bar itself. Colour bars can be displayed on the sounder screen, in this case on the extreme left of the screen. In the illustration, the colour bar or palette has been enlarged to make identification easier. This sounding was made in a dam with many old trees. The range was adjusted to show from the surface to the bottom, but since the main aim was to look for fish in mid water and among the trees, not a lot of the bottom trace was displayed and, also for this reason, a high sensitivity setting was used.

A-Scope is not the easiest display to learn to use, however once mastered the system will become an important part of any soundings. A mate of mine is a professional trap fisherman and has often said he would not have a sounder in his boat that did not have this facility.

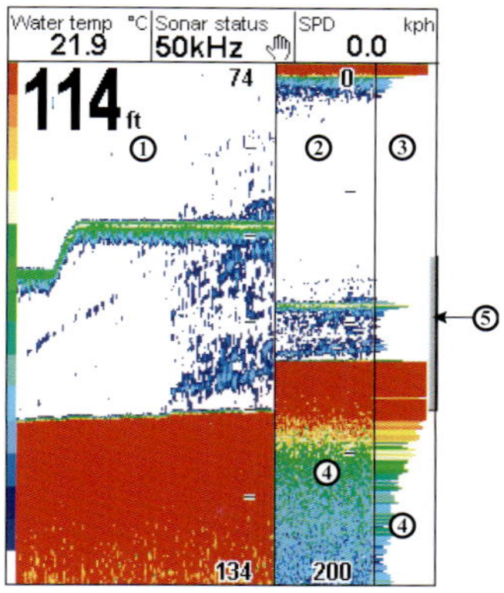

(Fig 35a) Late scatter on A-Scope
Three way split screen (1) 'zoomed' display, (2) 'surface to bottom' display and (3) 'A-Scope'. (4) Late scatter shown on the surface to bottom display and on the A-Scope. The A-Scope display clearly shows the subtle changes in colour as well as differences in signal strength of the late scatter. (5) is the bar that indicates the section of the water column that is zoomed.

Colour palettes

The colour palettes determine the range of colours used by the colour sounder to display echo returns of differing strengths. While most models and brands use a 16 colour range there may be minor differences in the actual shades used on any one particular sounder. These palettes are usually displayed for easy reference on one side or the bottom of the sounder screen, however the colour bar can also be removed from the screen if the operator so desires. This function is 'turned off' by means of menu. (Fig 36)

Usually the sounder's menu allows for selection of several 'standard' palettes. The main difference between these palettes is the colour used to depict the background, or zone of no signal returns. This may vary from white (clear), blue or black. Examples of these three background colours are shown in the illustrations throughout the book. The actual background chosen is largely a matter of personal taste, however the black background seems to work best when using the sounder at night.

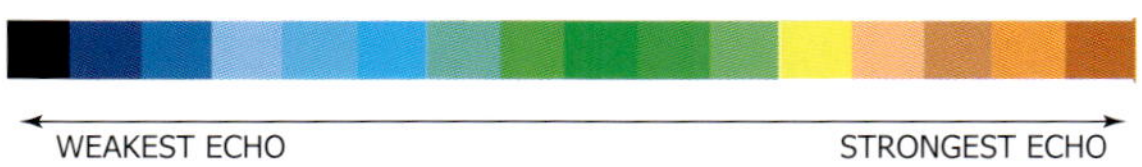

(Fig 36) Sixteen step colour palette
Most colour sounders use a range of 16 colours to display echoes of varying strengths. The range is known as a 'palette' and is usually displayed along the edge of the screen, although this feature may be turned off if not required.

Another variation in the palette selection is the facility to remove some of the colour bars from the display. For instance, the operator may choose to delete the two weakest echoes, that is, the two blues, from the display. This feature may be desirable if there were masses of small baitfish around, which could be obscuring the presence of larger fish. By eliminating the weaker echoes the larger fish will often show up. The actual menu selection may be called different features depending on brands and models, these include 'discrimination', 'noise suppression' or shown as a custom set-up.

Fish symbols

Displaying fish echoes as symbols or icons of fish is a relatively common sounder feature. The internal micro processor is programmed to display echoes as fish symbols if they meet certain criteria—the main one being that the echo is above and separated from the bottom sounding. This may also be called Fish Identification or more commonly just Fish ID. (Fig 37)

The fish symbol systems have a number of disadvantages and its use is not recommended. Some models display several sized icons to distinguish between small and large fish, however if there is a school of small baitfish clumped together, as baitfish naturally do, then the display will indicate a single icon for a large fish. Also, if there is any type of interference creating noise on the screen, then there is every chance at least some of this noise will be displayed as fish symbols. When surface clutter is strong, the operator can be presented with large fish icons swimming head-to-tail across the top of the screen, as the sounder converts the surface clutter into fish symbols.

Simulators

Most sounders are equipped with a simulator mode that enables the first time user to run a program that simulates the common functions of the sounder—such as shift, zoom, scroll speed, split screen, etc without having the boat on the water. While the simulator programs are helpful they do at times lead to some confusion by inexperienced operators as to what they can expect from their sounder in day to day operation. One display that creates problems is that of fish arches. This is addressed in the next chapter.

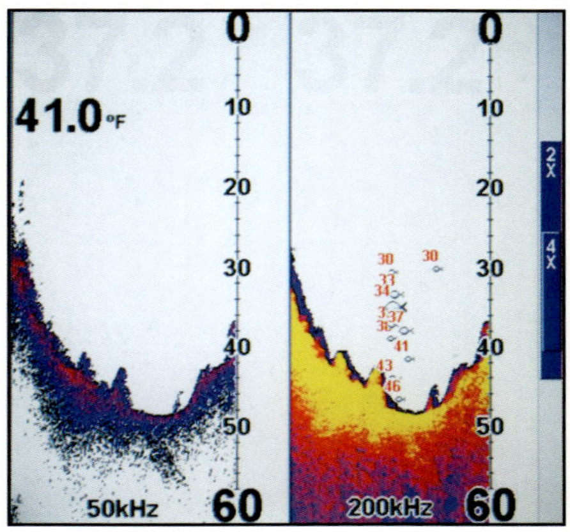

(Fig 37) Fish symbols
Fish symbols displayed on one of the many possible combinations of split screens available. Note that each symbol has been labelled with the depth of the particular fish.

Chapter six

Other Controls

Fish arches

Fish arches on the sounder display are formed when the boat passes over a fish in the water column directly below the boat, or when a fish swims below the boat, which must be stationary. If the fish only enters part of the beam, at A or C, a partial arch is formed, but if the fish moves through the centre of the beam the arch is fully formed.

The 'arched' shape is caused because the transducer beam is a cone. The distance at the edges of the cone is greater than at the centre and thus the fish appears to move upwards as it approaches the centre and moves downwards as it passes to the other edge of the beam. (Fig 38)

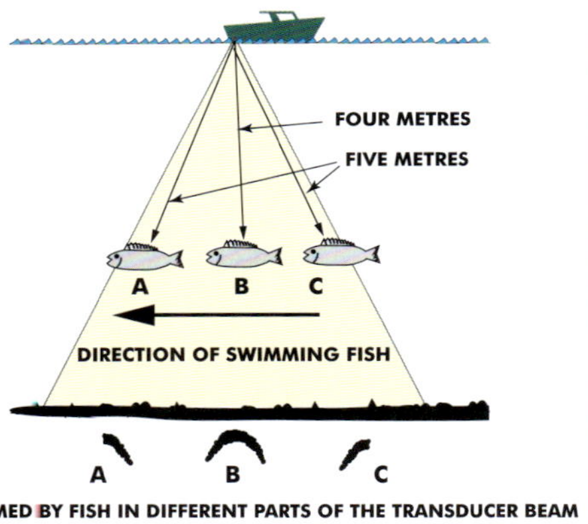

(Fig 38) Fish arches

The formation of fish arches on the sounder display is formed when the boat passes over a fish in the water column directly below the boat, or if a fish swims below the boat, which must be stationary. If the fish only enters part of the beam, points A and C, a partial arch is formed, but if the fish moves through the centre of the beam the arch is fully formed.

The arched shape is caused by the transducer beam being a cone, where the distance at the edges of the cone is greater than at the centre. Thus the fish appears to move upwards as it approaches the centre and moves downwards as it passes through the other edge of the beam.

The key word in the description of the formation of arches is the boat must be stationary or nearly so. This means if there is any wave motion moving the boat around, at best only a partial arch will be formed, most times none at all. Many anglers who fish regularly have never seen a fish arch and often are led to assume there is a problem with the positioning of the transducer, when in fact the only problem is having just the right conditions to form arches.

Speed and distance

Speed and distance readings (also know as a log) are a reasonably common function of sounders and uses a small paddle wheel, which is driven by water flow, and is an integral part of many transducers. Today, with GPS receivers becoming more common on even the smallest boats, the need for speed and distance data is not as great as it was previously, however there is one occasion when the water driven paddle wheel speed readings takes on a more significant roll.

When trolling lures and live baits, boat speed through the water becomes vital, however if there is any appreciable current the speed reading from the GPS can lead to appreciable errors due to the GPS indicating speed over the ground (SOG), not speed through the water. (Fig 39)

An occasion when trolling live slimy mackerel for marlin on the NSW north coast, the boat speed through the water was four knots, however the GPS was indicating SOG of half a knot in the opposite direction we were trolling. In other words there was a current running opposite our selected course and, had the boat speed been taken from the GPS, the bait would have been killed when towed through the water at eight and a half knots.

Total distance travelled is also a useful function, particularly for calculating such things as fuel consumption etc. (See also Fuel Monitoring)

(Fig 39) Speed & distance features

Many transducers are fitted with a paddle wheel, which measures both speed and distance through the water. The nylon line safety lanyard prevents the assembly being lost if the paddle is knocked off the transducer, a fairly common occurrence.

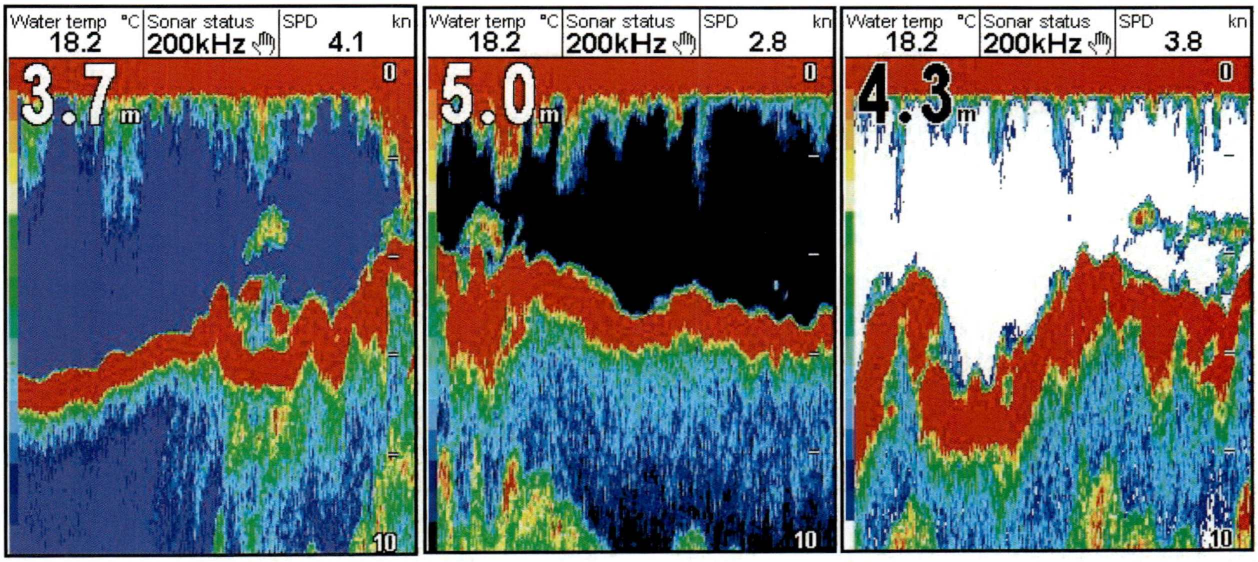

(Fig 40) Background colours (above)
The original colour video sounders traditionally used blue backgrounds and this is still the colour favoured by most users. However I have been using clear backgrounds for some time now and feel the absence of colour helps me to see small details, although the difference is minor at best and colour is a matter of taste... Although black may look stark for normal viewing, at night when the brightness control is turned down so as not to destroy the operator's night vision, the black background is a definite advantage.

Background colours

The original colour video sounders traditionally used blue backgrounds and this is still the colour favoured by most users. However, some operators find that a clear background with an absence of colour helps in noticing small details. The difference is minor at best and colour is a matter of taste.

Although black may look stark for normal viewing, at night when the brightness control is turned down so as not to destroy the operator's night vision, the black background is a definite advantage. (Fig 40)

White line

At one time, white line (also known as greyline) was featured on just about all sounders, however with the advent of multi-level displays for LCD monochrome sounders and colour units, the need for white line has lessened and today white line is rarely found. White line creates a thin space of white just below the top of the trace of the bottom, which enhances the difference between the true bottom and fish and other soft targets on or near the bottom. (Fig 41)

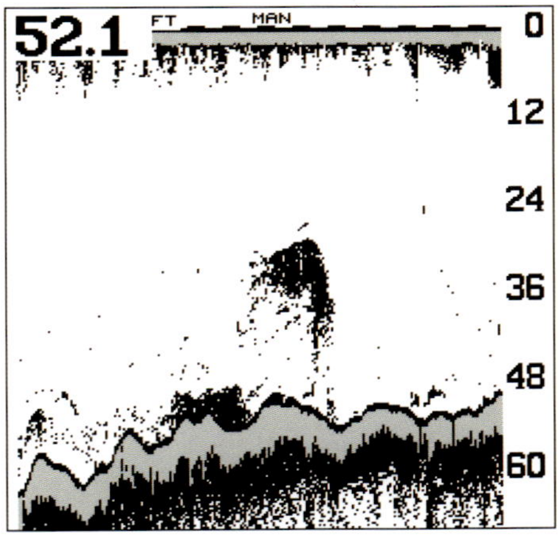

(Fig 41) White line or greyline
This image shows why greyline is so important in monochrome soundings. The images were made over a hard bottom with large concentrations of baitfish. Some of the bait is schooled-up above the bottom and others are down close to the bottom. The greyline on the Lowrance X-85 sounder has been correctly adjusted, separating the fish from the bottom. If you look closely at the bait pod in mid water you will notice there is a small amount of greyline in the centre of the pod. This is due to the baitfish being packed together so closely that the echo is almost as strong as the bottom echo.

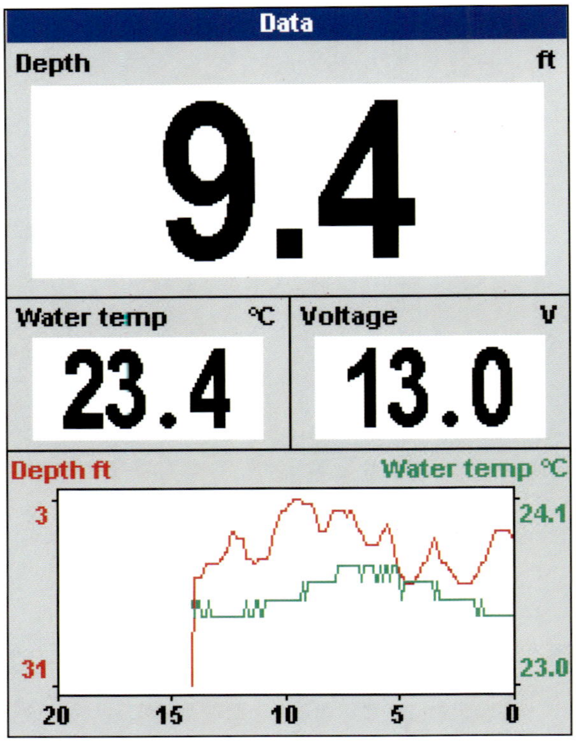

(Fig 42) Battery voltage display
Screen display showing, amongst other data the voltage of the boat's battery. This is a worthwhile feature in smaller boats with small motors that do not have a battery charging system (alternator). The display is often coupled to an audible alarm to alert the crew when the voltage drops to a critical level.

Battery voltage

Many sounders have the capability of displaying the voltage of the battery supplying current to the unit. This is a particularly desirable display when the sounder is used in boats fitted with comparatively small outboard motors not fitted with alternators capable of recharging the vessel's batteries. Often this type of installation uses a small gel type battery to power the sounder and the voltage display enables the operator to monitor the state of charge of the battery and indicates when charging is required. There is also an alarm that is activated when the voltage is approaching a critical level producing an audible tone as well as a visual symbol. (Fig 42)

Fuel monitoring

While monitoring of the boat's fuel supply and the rate the motor is using the fuel is not a common feature, it is available on some brands and models. As the trend towards integration of navigation, sounder and motor data continues, these monitors will be available as standard on more sounders.

Barometer

It is widely accepted weather conditions affect fish behaviour, particular barometric pressure changes. Humminbird's WeatherSense in an optional extra that displays, on the sounder screen, the current barometric pressure and a trend indicating increasing or decreasing barometric pressure over the last twelve hours. This information may be displayed as full screen or a digital readout. (Fig 43) (Fig 44)

(Fig 43)

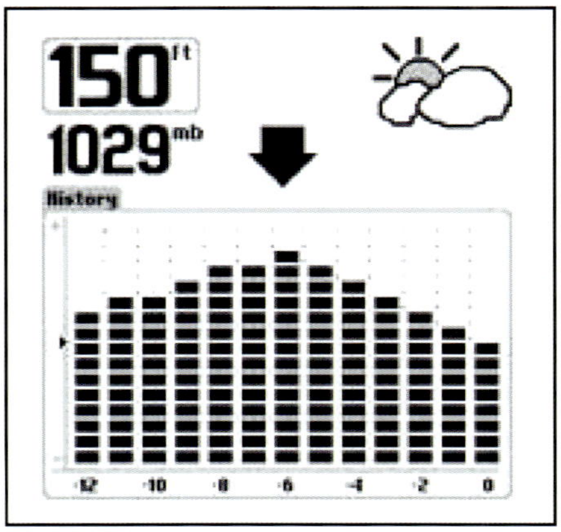

(Fig 44)

(Fig 43) & (Fig 44) Barometer
A barometric sensor is an add-on extra that records barometric changes in the weather and displays the changes on the sounder's screen.

Chapter seven

Interpreting Sounder Images

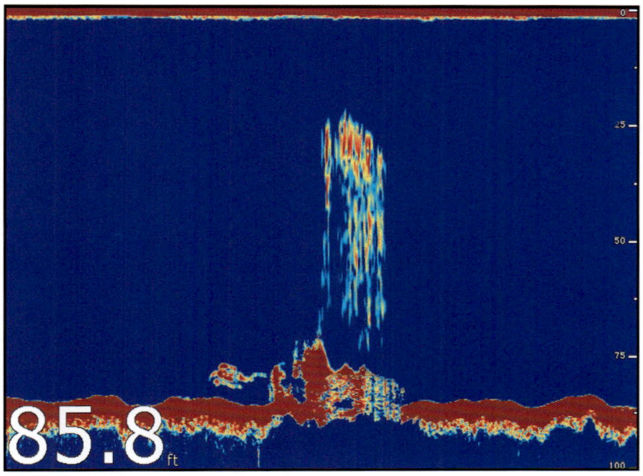

(Fig 45) Baitfish schools
A school of baitfish over a wreck that is situated on a sandy, featureless bottom. The elongated 'spire' shape of the school is typical of baitfish, in this case yellowtail scad, a species that is often found over bottom features such as structures and reefs.

While it is all very good understanding the functions of a sounder and being proficient in adjusting the controls to get the perfect picture, in the end it all comes down to one thing—understanding the images on the screen and perceiving what they actually represent. Of course, one needs to be able to effectively operate the sounder to obtain soundings that will enable you to identify fish, but if you cannot recognise them, then all the theory is for nothing.

To become accomplished at fish identification takes lots and lots of practice. There is no easy shortcut, you just have to keep looking at soundings and relating them to the fish you are pulling on board, until it becomes second nature. Just about every species of fish has a distinct signature echo, so it is important to learn to read these signatures. The illustrations will give you an insight into reading soundings, but be aware the location and water conditions may change the appearance of some fish echoes.

There are some basic rules that will help, but this is only the beginning. It is practice—in the boat, out on the water—which will hone your skills in identifying fish and structures. A fact worth noting at this stage is that characteristic echoes may vary from location to location. You may become expert at identifying fish on your home dam or lake or on your offshore reefs, but move a few hundred miles away and you are faced with a whole new ball game.

The most basic fish echo, and arguably the most important, is that of baitfish, for where there are baitfish, sooner or later the predators will be along. Baitfish schools fall into a couple of basic shapes that are universal to just about all baitfish. Since it is a fact of baitfish life that they will be chased and if caught, eaten, they tend to form into dense schools for self protection, with those on the outside jockeying to try to get closer to the centre of the school. This survival technique makes distinctive echoes that are easy to recognise.

Around structures and bottom features, baitfish tends to congregate in a spire type of school which, depending on the number of fish, may be many metres high. (Fig 45)

Bait schools may be so densely packed that on a monochrome sounder they will display as a black blob, but if the greyline is adjusted correctly, the fish schools will appear black and the bottom will greyline, marking a clear distinction between the fish and the bottom. There will be occasions when the schools of bait are so dense that some greylining may take place in the centre of the school, but this is obvious, in fact it tends to indicates just how much bait there is in the school. (Fig 46 and Fig 47)

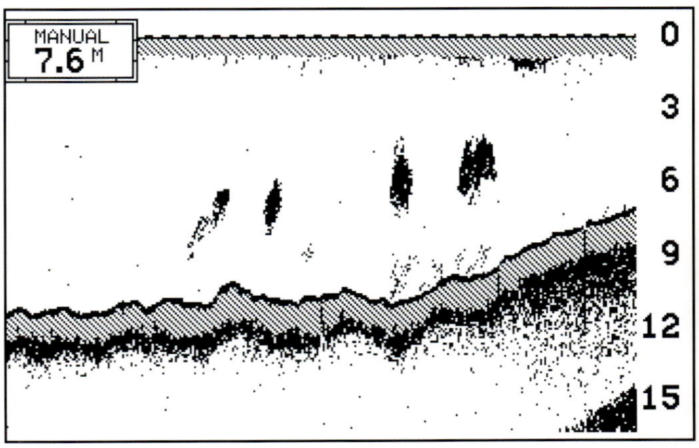

(Fig 46) Baitfish schools formed in open water
These are the identifying school shapes of baitfish in open water. They are schools of slimy mackerel, a common summer baitfish much favoured by marlin and yellowtail kingfish.

A colour sounder will generally display the bait in blues and greens but in the case of very dense schools will show yellow and even red in the centre. Often baitfish will school together in open water and form what is aptly called bait balls, these balls may be spherical or shaped like a rugby ball. Study the accompanying illustrations and you will have a good idea of how bait shows on a sounder screen. (Fig 48)

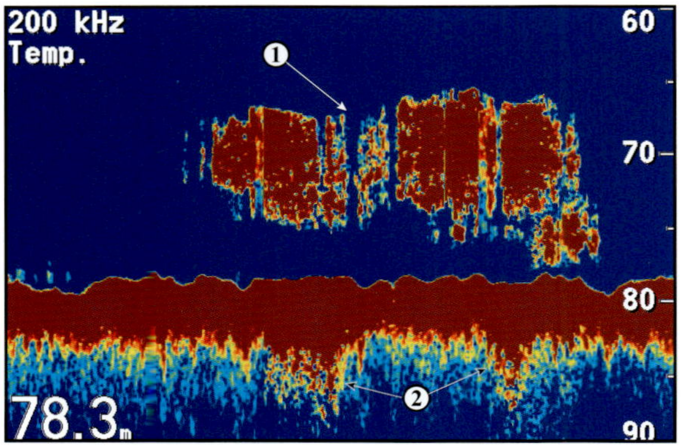

(Fig 47) Bait ball
(1) A large bait ball suspended well off the bottom. These fish were cowan young, species closely related to the yellowtail scad, which move along the NSW coast in autumn. The apparent gaps in the school are caused by the narrow transducer beam and the motion of the boat. The school was so dense they are causing a late scatter effect (2) to show below the bottom trace.

4/05/2007 9:34:29 am	
POSITION *33°17'485* *E 151°43'927*	***SELECTED FREQ*** *200 50 BOTH* *200 kHz*
COG *257°M*	***AUTO GAIN*** *LO MED HI* *MANUAL 54%*
SOG *3.9 kts*	
DEPTH *78.3 m*	
BATTERY *14.2V*	***TEMPERATURE*** *19.3°C*

When a screen download is created in the Raymarine system, a text file is also saved and attached to the downloaded file with the information shown below. The position, COG (course over ground) and SOG (speed over ground), is derived from the GPS, while the depth, temperature, selected frequency, gain and battery voltage is from the sounder.

The second example, (Fig 49) is an interesting sounding and quite an unexpected one. We were running a downrigger, which we decided to lift up a little towards the surface, when the wire became tangled and jammed on the downrigger drum. The boat was stopped while the tangle was cleared and just before we started up again we noticed the sounder and recorded the display.

On the left of the screen is the trace of the downrigger bomb being lifted and then stopping when the jam occurred. At this point there are very few fish on the screen and the boat is stopped. (There was virtually no wind and very little drift). As time went on baitfish began to appear on the screen aggregating around the bomb. Most of the fish echoes appear to be vertical, suggesting the fish have moved towards the bomb parallel to the bottom, had they moved up, or down, in the water column, the echoes would have been slanted. While I can draw no worthwhile conclusions from this sounding, it does illustrate how much information is contained in soundings if you know how to read them. When this sounding was made the unit was operating with the 50 kHz frequency, wide beam and in split screen mode with A-scope.

The sounding made in the Peter Faust Dam in north Queensland shows a good display of baitfish amongst the drowned trees. While there was no indication of larger fish, the presence of the bait in and around the cover encouraged us to cast in among the dead trees, and Yvonne was rewarded with a nice barra. (Fig 50 and Fig 51)

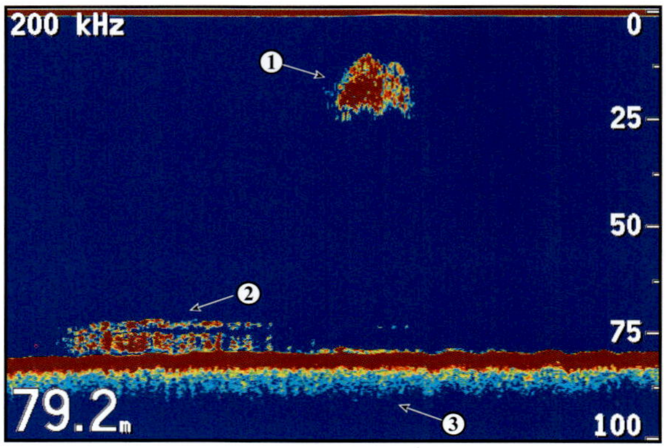

(Fig 48) Mid-water bait
(1)This bait ball is slimy mackerel, a prime offshore, summer bait, particularly for game fish such as marlin. The rounded shape the ball takes on is typical of baitfish schools in open water well away from the bottom, unlike the bait (2) down close to the bottom, which are probably nannygai. Slimy mackerel are basically a surface to mid-water species and nannygai are bottom dwellers. Note the lack of late scatter (3) below the bottom trace, which indicates a sandy bottom.

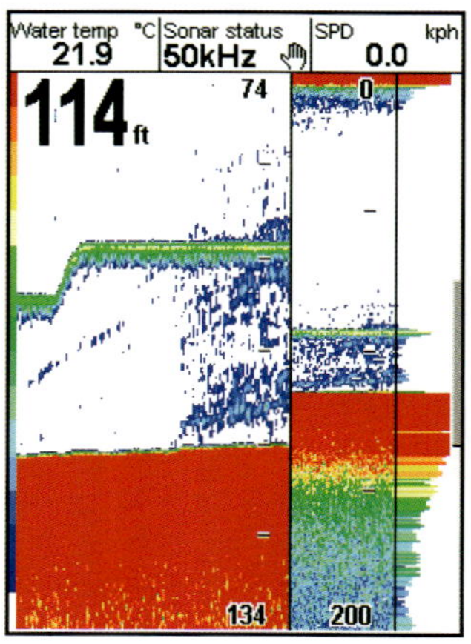

(Fig 49) Baitfish congregating around a downrigger bomb
Baitfish gather around a stationary downrigger weight. Note the split screen displaying zoomed view, standard surface to bottom view and A-Scope. By splitting the screen into these views it is possible to see a total overview of the water column, a close-up view of the downrigger bomb and the advantages of A-Scope.

(Fig 50) & (Fig 51) Baitfish amongst heavy timber
Several concentrated schools of bait amongst the dead trees in the Peter Faust Dam in Far North Queensland. While no large fish are showing in the sounding, the presence of baitfish encouraged repeated lure casting in and around the sunken timber, which produced a nice barra and several other fish that were lost amongst the dead trees that abound in the dam.

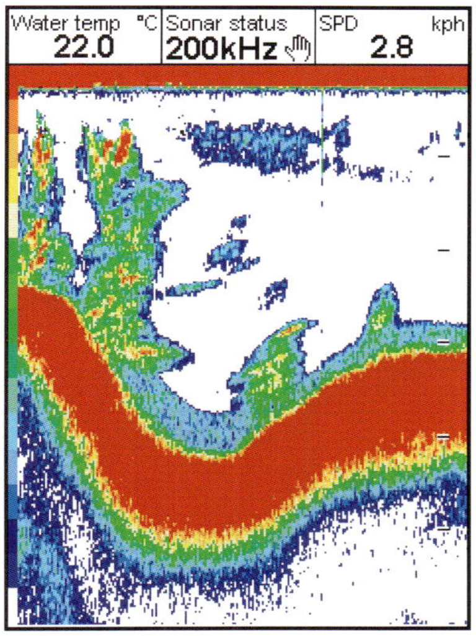

(Fig 51)

(Fig 50)

Often relating the sounder images to surface features can be helpful in creating a mental picture of the underwater scene and how the sounder will display it. (Fig 52)

The picture of the tops of dead trees above the water indicated snags below the surface. The sounding was made with the boat running close to the snags and confirmed the presence of old drowned trees, but they appeared to be cut off well below the surface. (Fig 53) However, the illustration of the transducer beam explains the apparent anomaly. The transducer beam close to the surface is narrow and it is not until the beam widens out sufficiently before it starts recording the trees. It is just a case of applying the theory of transducer beam angles to practical situations. (Fig 54)

To generate soundings of this kind—soundings that show a wealth of detail—the first step is to make sure the unit is operating in the manual mode. The gain, or sensitivity, should be adjusted to maximum for the prevailing conditions. To do this increase the gain until 'noise' starts to appear on the screen, then just back the gain off until there is just a suggestion of clutter on the screen. This method ensures maximum gain, which guarantees no small details are lost. Then manually adjust the range to position the bottom trace in the lower third of the screen. This will give some room beneath the bottom to indicate late scatter, which is so important in determining bottom hardness.

Fig 52, Fig 53 and Fig 54 Drowned trees above and below the surface
The surface picture of the tops of dead trees contrasts with the sounding of trees below the dam's surface. The sounding shows the trees cut-of before their tops reach the surface, which appears to be an anomaly as the boat was right alongside the trees when the sounding was recorded. However, the diagram shows the first part of the transducer's cone angle near the surface where the beam is narrowest and 'missing' the trees, but as the cone widens out the sounder 'sees' the trees and displays them on the screen.

Fig 52

Fig 53

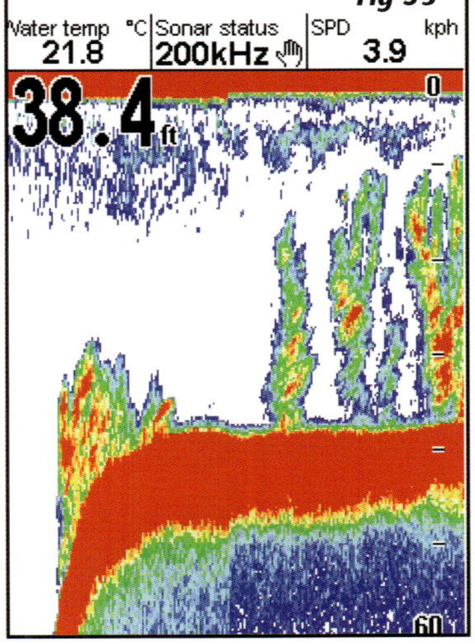

Fig 54

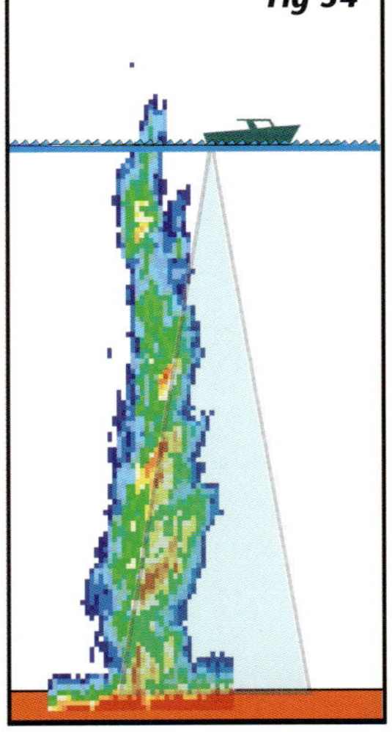

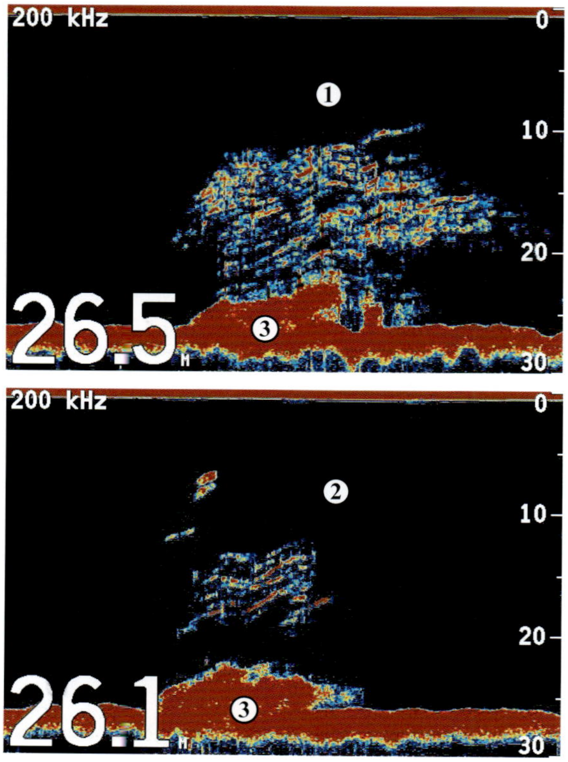

(Fig 55) The effect of gain settings on baitfish displays
These are two soundings are of baitfish hanging over a wreck off Pittwater on the NSW coast. The first pass over the wreck (1) showed a large mass of bait, yellowtail scad, with indications of larger fish. Before the second pass (2) the sensitivity was reduced to show only the larger fish in the bait school. Since the boat did not precisely follow the same track, the sounding of the wreck is a slightly different shape in the two soundings. However, because the DSP system adjusted the sensitivity of this part of the sounding (3), the display of the wreck and the bottom is of the same density in both soundings, despite the different settings of the sensitivity control.

The previous paragraph refers to manually setting the sensitivity using a standard sounder, however adjusting this control on a sounder using Digital Signal Processing (DSP) is a little different as this system tends to suppress noise making for cleaner looking pictures. Also, the sensitivity is adjusted automatically for the various sections of the sounding—bottom, fish, baitfish etc. This makes the finding the 'correct' sensitivity position a little less critical. I find the best method is to observe the subject I am most interested in—baitfish, bottom texture, structures etc and adjust the gain for best display and the rest of the display tends to look after itself. (Fig 55)

While on the subject of auto controls, make sure the Fish ID feature is turned off.

These are the basics of fish identification as well as the identification of other underwater features that are displayed on the sounder screen. To become a competent operator, one needs to observe closely just what the sounder is displaying and then relate this feature to conditions you have seen and identified before—remember, practice, practice, practice. For example, if there is a big school of baitfish showing, drop a bait jig down and catch a few, commit the echoes appearance to memory and next time you spot this type of echo you will have a pretty good idea of the species showing on the sounder.

Local knowledge also plays a big part in this learning experience. While there is a certain similarity between fish echoes many areas have different conditions and species which tend to produce displays that are unique to the area.

Customised display

With so many features available it is almost impossible to have all of these displayed on the sounder screen at any one time, to do so would result in a meaningless jumble of data and leave little space for the actual sounding. Since not all users need to access all of these attributes at the same time, it is possible to customise the screen to display as few or as many as required. Also, multiple screens can be programmed for different operating conditions and locations and each customised screen can be recalled by the touch of a menu key when required. (Fig 56)

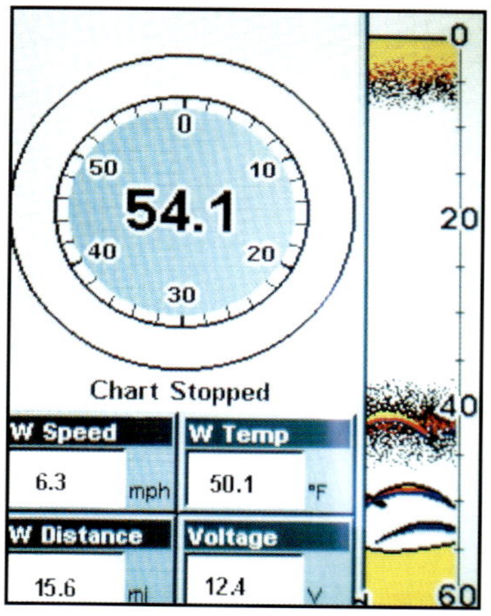

(Fig 56) Customised display
The display on the Lowrance X100C has been customised to only display the boat speed, the distance the boat has travelled (a log), water temperature and the battery voltage. This image was a simulated display and the screen was frozen to prevent movement interfering with the photograph. The clock-like display is a modern presentation of the original flasher sounder and is a similar to A-Scope, giving a real time sounder reading. Unfortunately with the chart stopped, the echo flashers are not displayed. The small window on the right is a 'standard' sounding display. The digital depth display in the centre of the 'clock' is the actual bottom depth.

Chapter eight

Recent Innovations

(Fig 57) Humminbird 987C SI

Humminbird's first side imaging sounder, the 987C SI

Several new systems, which will dramatically change the way sounders are used in the future have become available in recent years to view the underwater world.

Side Scan or Side Imaging

A completely new sounding system for recreational fishers is Side Scan sonar or Side Imaging, which is Humminbird's proprietary name for what is a type of side scanning sonar. Side scan sounding is used extensively in underwater searches for wrecks, crashed aircraft etc, as well as bottom profiling. The commercial side scan sonar uses a towed transmitter and receiver encased in a hydrodynamically shaped drone known as a tow fish'. A transducer array is mounted on both sides of the drone that sends and receives sound pulses. The transducer beam is quite wide in the vertical plane but extremely narrow, (typically one degree) in the horizontal plane. The sound pulses are transmitted at a very rapid rate and 'paint' a continuous oblique image of the bottom features for a considerable distance either side of the tow fish. The data from the drone is digitised and transmitted, via a cable, to computers on the tow vessel.

Side Imaging

Humminbird's side imaging system uses a special transducer to produce images of the bottom on either side of the boat, producing 'pictures' that are more like conventional photographs than sounder images. While the side imaging system it is not really a fish finder as such, although it will display fish echoes, it is a technique to find and display bottom details with unparalleled clarity and detail. Humminbird's first side imaging unit, the 987c SI and the later 797C2, (Fig 57 and Fig 58) uses a special transducer mounted on the boat and projects a wide sound beam to both sides and at right angles to the boat's direction of travel (Fig 15). As in side scan systems the beam is wide in the vertical plane and very narrow horizontally, less than 2 degrees for the 455 kHz and 3 degrees for 262 kHz frequency. By eliminating the need to tow a drone, the whole system becomes much simpler and can be used on just about any boat.

It does take time and practice to operate the unit efficiently and recognise what one is actually seeing on the screen, also there are a number of mechanical considerations that are somewhat different from the 'traditional' sounder. First is the positioning of the transducer. Because of the very wide beam angle, finding a suitable position on the transom to mount the transducer takes a little bit of forethought and perhaps some trial and error. For transducer installation on a mono hull a satisfactory position on the transom can generally be found, even though it still may be necessary to tilt the outboard motor up a little when actually sounding in the side imaging mode. For the serious operator a through-hull transducer installation eliminates all of these problems.

***(Fig 58) Humminbird 797C**2*

The latest side imaging sounder in the Humminbird's stable. The 797C2 uses 455 kHz, 200 kHz and 83 kHz frequencies. When the 83 kHz frequency is used while side imaging, the lower frequency allows depths of up to 50 metres to be scanned. It also enhances the detail in the shallower water.

Understanding side imaging displays

Side imaging displays are an entirely different presentation of the underwater scene to traditional soundings. There are a number of differences between 'ordinary' sounding and side imaging displays. First, the screen scrolls from the top of the screen to the bottom, second, the surface trace runs down the centre of the screen, not along the top. The display is mono (not colour) and there are currently three choices available of the screen colour—grey, green and blue. Blue is the default colour and is in most conditions the best choice, although this is a personal thing, which may not suit all tastes.

Finally, the image is inverted to what one would expect from a 'black and white' image. That is, the strongest echoes are shown lightest, and weak or absence of echoes is darkest, as in a black and white photograph, so the water column above the bottom shows dark blue. However, once these differences are grasped the display reveals a wealth of information.

Shadows play a very important part in interpreting side images. If one imagines standing at night, some height above your surroundings and then shining a strong spot light across the terrain to your left and right. Objects such as dead trees and clumps of rocks will be highlighted and cast distinctive shadows that help to define them, this then is not too different to the screen images you can expect to see in side imaging mode. (Fig 59)

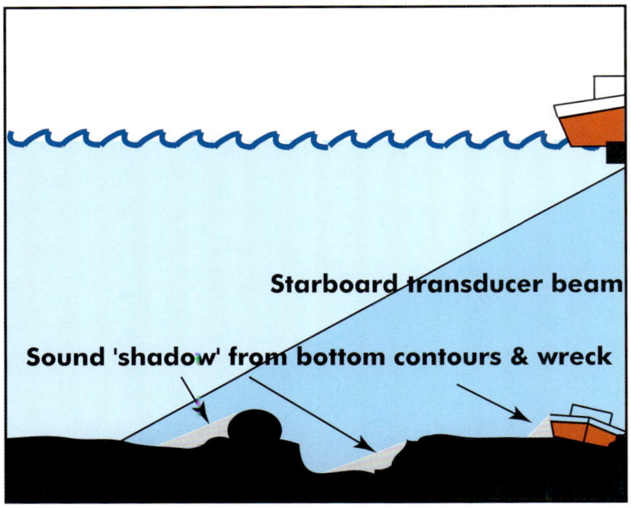

(Fig 59) Side imaging transducer's beams

This is a graphical representation of the transducer beam's coverage in side and top views on Humminbird's 987 side imaging sounder. The lower frequency 262 kHz beam produces the widest coverage while the higher frequency 455 kHz beam gives maximum definition. The new 797 model uses an 83 kHz frequency for even greater coverage, making side imaging practical to greater depths than ever before.

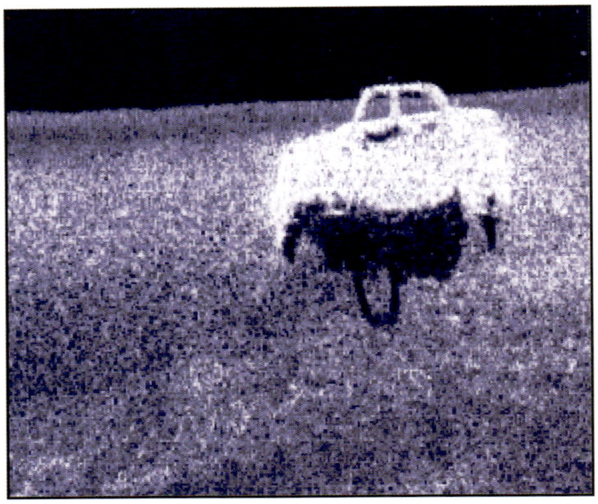

(Fig 60) Side image of a car

The side image of a car dumped in a creek leaves no doubt as to what the object really is. This old car was evidently dumped in a local creek and was stumbled across unexpectedly, however it does demonstrate the capability of the system to locate structures and bottom features.

As in our example, shadows are formed by the lack of reflected sound surfaces in the area of the beam. Shadows can be a very valuable as an interpretative tool by indicating more about the makeup of the object than the reflected sonar itself. Shadows add the three dimensional quality to the image and indicating orientation of the object. Shadows provide strong clues of an object's actual shape and highlight depressions and hillocks on the bottom.

The reflective material of the target and the bottom area determine the intensity of the sonar return. Rocks and gravel provide a better sound return than mud and sand due to the density (to sound) of the objects. Upper facing slopes facing the transducer are better reflectors than downward slopes because of angle at which the beam strikes the bottom.

When using side imaging, chart, or scroll, speed and boat speed are important factors. The default chart speed is mid range and this is ideal for most sounding. Humminbird suggest boat speed be from 2 to 6 mph (3 to 10 km/hr), remembering that in deeper water, slower boat speed will produce better images.

To realise the full potential of the system it is important the side imaging process be understood and a study of the images will help to grasp the concept and serve to illustrate the potential of the system. The sounding of a car that had been dumped in a local creek is a good example of side imaging. I came across the car when travelling along the creek, but there was no mistaking what the image was. (Fig 60) Finding and identifying structures, drowned trees, wrecks, in fact any bottom features is easy using this technology

Being a relatively new system it is reasonable to expect that in the foreseeable future the system will become more refined and develop into a common tool for serious fishermen.

Digital Signal Processing (DSM)

Raymarine launched a new system to digitally process the returning echo from a transducer, which they called HD Digital (High Definition Digital). The HD Digital system was first released as an 'add-on' module for their large screen sounders. They then adapted the system for their smaller sounders, such as the DS500X and DS600X (125 mm and 150 mm diagonal screen sizes), which are stand alone units and the A65 plotter sounder, which uses a 'black box' module, designated DSM25, which is fitted between the sounder and the transducer. (Fig 61)

The DSM25 module varies the bandwidth of the returning echo pulse several thousand times a second. To help understand HD Digital, remember that a normal sounder produces a transmit pulse it is at a fixed frequency, usually 200 or 50 kilohertz (a kilohertz is a thousand cycles per second). However, the pulse is not exactly that frequency, for instance at a 200 kHz nominal frequency, the pulse may span 190 kHz to 210 kHz—this range of 20 kHz is the 'bandwidth' of the transmitted pulse. A narrow bandwidth gives good definition and a wide bandwidth makes for a stronger return. The actual bandwidth selected by designers for a 'standard' sounder is a compromise between definition and strong echo returns.

(Fig 61) Raymarine's A65 Sounder/Plotter
Raymarine's sounder which when fitted with the optional extra 'black box', the DSM25, converts to a high definition digital unit which is capable of producing outstanding images.

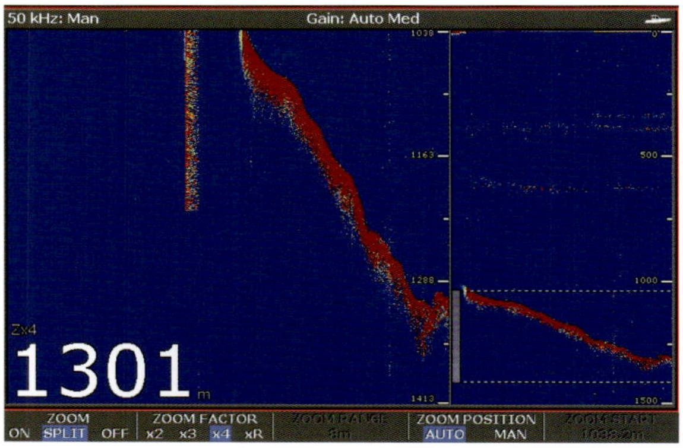

(Fig 62) Deep water sounding
An advantage of the high definition digital technology is the superior deep water performance. This impressive download of a split image screen shows strong bottom echoes in 1301 metres (4265 feet) of water. The frequency was 50 kHz and the sounder power was one kilowatt (1000 watts), a very modest power output for water this deep.

(Fig 63) Furuno FCV 620A
Furuno's high definition system is called Digital Signal Processing (DSP) and is used in the FCV 620A.

The HD Digital system samples each tiny part of the returning echo and adjusts the bandwidth of the receiver to provide optimal bandwidth for that part of the echo. Not only does the DSM adjust the bandwidth to suit each section of the echo, but it also varies the gain (sensitivity) of each part of signal, in fact there are over 220 parameters within the echo pulse that are adjusted each second.

One of these parameters is Time Variable Gain (TVG), which is a parameter used to control surface clutter. Look closely at the HD digital images and notice there is no surface clutter, just a narrow zero surface line. Another advantage is deep water performance, which is enhanced in no small way by the constantly adjusting gain. (Fig 62)

Furuno have also released their high definition digital system, called DSP (Digital Signal Processing), which has been incorporated in their two sounders, the FCV-585 FCV-620. (Fig 63) The FCV-620 is a 135 mm diagonal screen and has a 600 watt RMS output. The DSP operates on similar lines to the Raymarine's system and adjusts among other parameters gain, STC, output power and sounding rate. Furuno state the adjustment of the sounding rate (sounding rate is the number of transmitted sound pulses per second), is as high as 3000 times a second when the sounder is operating in shallow water, to produce excellent definition of bait pods and individual fish. (Fig 55)

Lowrance have recently begun marketing their high definition system, called 'Optimiser', which is a separate add-on accessory fitted in the transducer cable between the sounder display unit and the transducer. (Fig 64)

I feel the high definition digital systems are a genuine breakthrough in sounder technology, the impact of which is equal to, if not greater than that of LCD displays. The system is producing high quality displays of amazing quality and as other manufacturers follow suit we will see more units coming on the market using this technology as well as fine tuning and improvements to the existing sounders and the inevitable reduction in prices. (Fig 65)

Integration

While integration has been around in one form or another for some time, it is becoming more commonplace. The system enables single units, such as sounders, to be integrated with other units into a single system rather than each single item functioning alone. Integration systems may also be called 'networks' and basically link various electronic equipment together to a single display or to share the various functions available with other equipment e.g. plotters, temperature etc. Raymarine's system is called 'Seatalk high speed network', which is a single cable connecting together chartplotters, sounders, radar, video, instrumentation data of all kinds including engine data. Furuno's system using computer Ethernet oriented technology and is call Navnet. Electronic monitoring of engine parameters promises to feature very big in future integrated systems, both for large inboard installations and outboards. Mercury and Navman have developed an engine monitoring system called 'SmartCraft', which seems to be setting the standard for this technology, but other companies are developing similar products, many of which will be released as standard on new engines or as add-on features.

Obviously these monitoring systems apply to larger boats but already there are integrated systems ideally suited to small craft. Navman have, as standard, on many of their sounders provision for fuel monitoring, all that is needed is the addition of inexpensive flow meter in the engine fuel line. The fuel information displayed includes the fuel used, the fuel remaining, flow rate in litres per hour, the economy at the present speed, the boat speed and the range at the current boat speed with the remaining fuel.

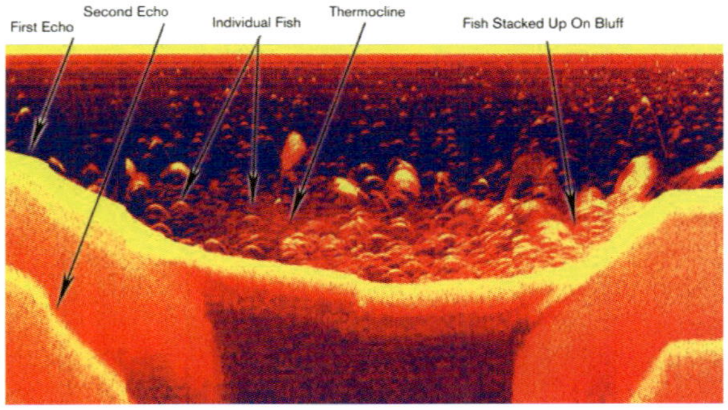

(Fig 64) Lowrance Optimiser

Download of Lowrance's Digital Signal Processor called 'Optimiser'. The optimiser is an add-on black box fitted between the sounder and the transducer.

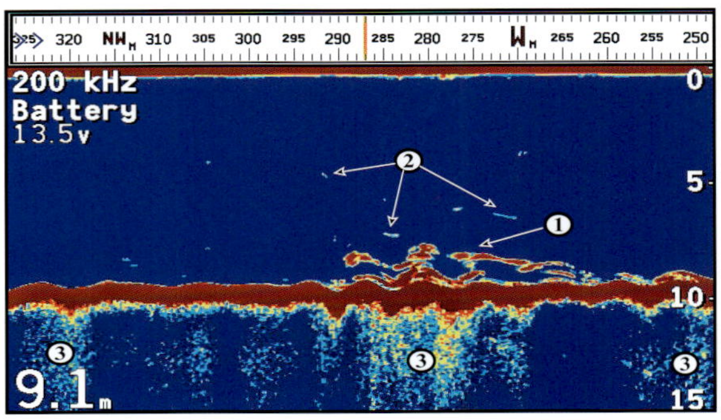

(Fig 65) Digital signal processing in Lake Macquarie

This sounding was made in Lake Macquarie, a large salt water lake on the NSW central coast, using a Raymarine A65 sounder. The fish (1) are mulloway, about 3 kg in size, schooling over a small patch of hard ground that is surrounded by soft mud in the lake. The area of hard bottom is indicated by the late scatter (3) and (4).

In the relatively shallow water, the fish are easily spooked by outboard motors. Consequently we usually stop the motor some distance away and drift with wind over the spot. When this download was taken the boat was ghosting along at 0.6 knots, which accounts for the somewhat 'stretched' look of the fish, both the mulloway and the few baitfish (2). We had sounded over this location a few hours earlier but found few baitfish and no larger fish (5), however once the sun had set the mulloway moved in providing us with a good evening's fishing.

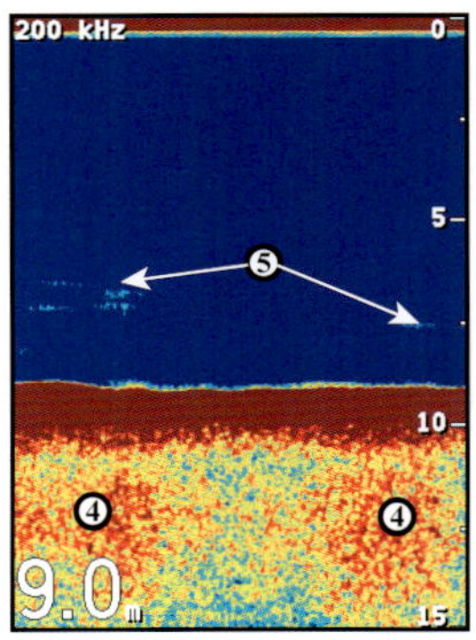

All of these examples are proprietary systems, that is, the senders and information is tailored to suit one brand and cannot be used on any other brand units. However, there is a system that is available to all manufacturers for transmitting data around the boat, known as NMEA network protocol. This protocol has been around for a long time—over 25 years. However the protocol, known as NMEA 0183 (the number indicates when the protocol was drawn up e.g. 1983), became almost universally excepted for data transfer, but due to the rapid expansion of marine electronics, the protocol is unable to handle the sheer quantity of data produced by modern equipment. An updated version, NMEA 2000, has been drawn up and is now starting to appear in equipment, including sounders. This NMEA 2000 protocol can handle just about any requirement needed to transfer data around the boats system, except video and full sounder displays, that is each sounder display requires its own separate transducer.

The latest sounders from Lowrance have been designed to access and distribute data from GPS, engine gauges etc and display it on the sounder screens. Lowrance calls their system 'LowranceNet'. (Fig 66) More and more manufacturers will use this system in the future as it is simple to install and relatively cheap.

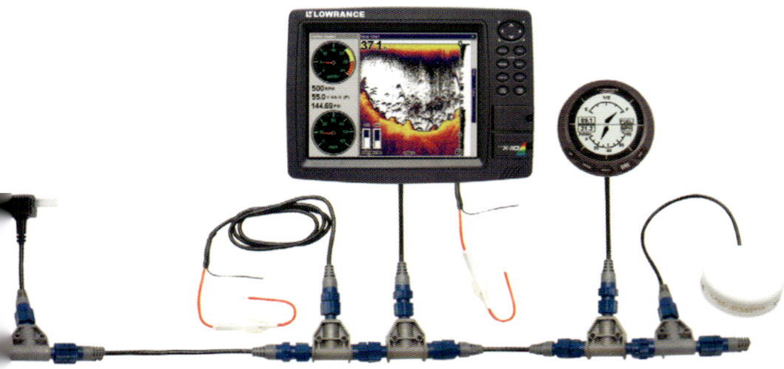

(Fig 66) LowranceNet sample setup
The Lowrance integration system called LowranceNet uses the NMEA 2000 protocol.

Combo units

Today there are a number of combo units available from most of the recognised brands. A combo unit is a sounder and GPS plotter combined in the one case and sharing the same screen and many anglers are faced with question of would it be better to buy a combo unit or separate sounder and plotter.

There are a number of factors to consider. First is the question of space, particularly dashboard space, on which to mount the unit or units. If you have little room to play with, then the combos are often the way to go.

Another consideration is cost, as a rule the combo units are cheaper than a separate sounder and plotter.

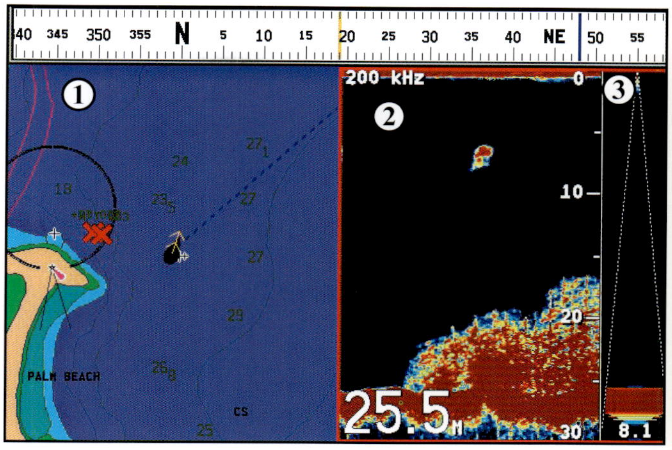

(Fig 67) Combo display
A combo display of a GPS chart plotter and sounder that illustrates the versatility of this type of equipment. The display (1) on the left is the chart of the area—Palm Beach Pittwater, North of Sydney. The chart has a wreck symbol and the boat's icon in position over the wreck. The middle screen (2) is the sounder, which is showing the wreck and the baitfish. The narrow display (3) is a graphic presentation of the transducer's cone angle and the area covered on the bottom by the beam, known as the footprint of the transducer. The circle covered by the transducer in this case is 8.1 metres.

A few years ago the tendency was for more compact sounders and plotters, which led to smaller screen sizes and as a result the combo screens were often quite cluttered. However today the trend has reversed and larger screens are now the norm, allowing more room on the screen to display the data and images from both systems.

I feel two separate dedicated units is the best option, as each unit can be set up to perform at its best, however at the end of the day it is very much a personal choice when all the other factors are taken into consideration. I fitted a combo unit to my small runabout as available space was the prime, overriding consideration in this case and I am using a combo unit on the 6.5 metre cat used as a test rig. (Fig 67)

Memory cards

A feature that has appeared on sounders in recent years is memory cards. (Fig 68) This facility enables the operator to download or 'dump' screen images directly to an integral electronic memory card—the same type of cards used in digital cameras. Like digital photographs, these sounder images can be uploaded into a computer and then viewed and printed out.

Many anglers will probably never use this feature, however it does offer a number of advantages. When screen images are viewed on the boat there is usually insufficient time to view all the details of the sounding.

By recording these sounding one can view them at a later date, either on the computer screen or in the form of colour prints. The advantage is one can study these images at leisure and it is amazing the extra details and subtleties contained in the soundings that would be missed when viewed on the sounder screen when the boat is on the water.

(Fig 68) Memory cards
Two of the most common memory cards used by sounder manufactures to download data and screen displays. The right hand card is a SD (secure digital) type and the other is MMC (multi media card). Some units can use both types of cards.

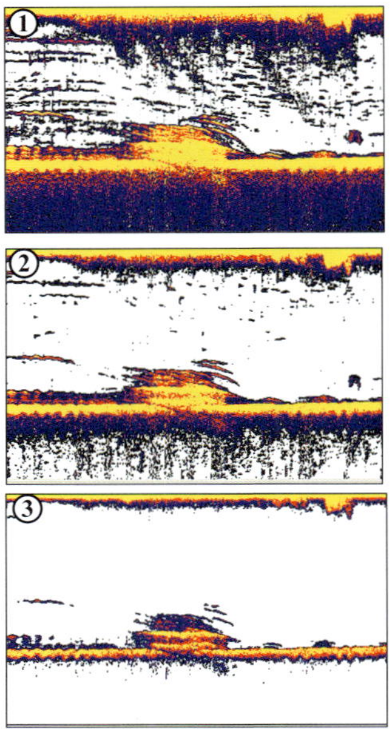

(Fig 69)
Lowrance Sonar view
The Lowrance system records the display as continuous video type mode. (Others brands generally record the screen in a snapshot mode). The data is saved to a memory card, either MMC or SD, and can be downloaded to a computer and displayed using software called 'SonarView' that can be downloaded, free of charge, from the Lowrance website.
Not only can the whole of the recording be re-viewed just as it was recorded, but the display can be frozen at any point for detailed examination.
One of the really useful innovations of the system is one can play 'What if' with the display, changing the sensitivity and colour line settings just as if you were out on the water adjusting the actual sounder controls. This is tremendously helpful to evaluate just what effect these adjustments would have made to the sounding. In this case the sensitivity is varied for the same sounding.

(Fig 70) Sonarview
A computer screen download of the SonarView software display. The on-screen slider controls (1) for adjusting sensitivity and colorline are at the bottom of the screen.

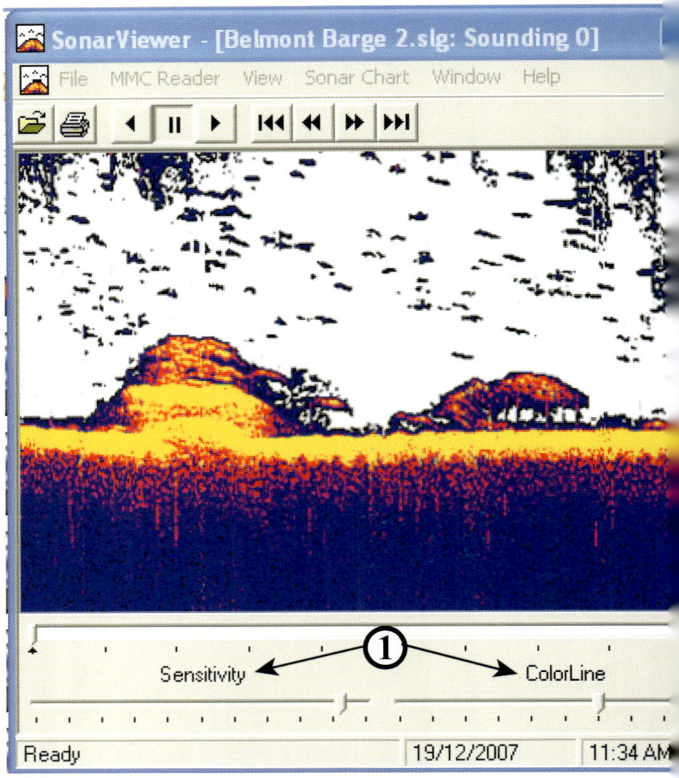

Lowrance uses a system that records the display as continuous video type mode. (Others brands generally record the screen in a snapshot mode). The data is saved to a memory card, either MMC (multi media card) or SD (secure digital), and can be downloaded to a computer and displayed using software called 'SonarView' that can be downloaded, free of charge, from the Lowrance website.

Not only can the whole of the recording be re-viewed just as it was recorded, but also the display can be frozen at any point for detailed examination. But one of the really useful innovations of the system is one can play 'What if' with the display, changing the sensitivity and colour line settings just as if you were out on the water adjusting the actual sounder controls. This is tremendously helpful to evaluate just what effect these adjustments would have made to the sounding. (Fig 69 and Fig 70)

Sounder screen downloads of real, on-the-water soundings are also invaluable for illustrating articles and how-to instruction sheets and have a real place in modern sounders.

Chapter nine

Sounder Installation

Installation of modern sounders is in reality a pretty straightforward job. One does not need to be a rocket scientist to undertake the task, just have a reasonable level of DIY skills and a few tools most handymen would have in their tool kits. Fortunately, the vast majority of sounders on today's market have simple-to-follow comprehensive manuals. The first thing to do is to sit down and read the manual and then plan in your mind how you are going to apply it.

The single most important part of any sounder installation is the correct fitting of the transducer. Over 70 per cent of sounder problems can be traced back to incorrect fitting of the transducer, so take your time and do the job properly—you will reap the benefits for years to come.

Transom mount transducers

While there are several different types of installations of transducers, such as through-hull and in-hull, transom mounted is by far the most common installation. The majority of modern sounders use a 'triducer', which combines a transducer element, a temperature sensor and a paddle wheel for speed readings. For simplicity, the word 'transducer' will be used for both triducers and transducers. Some manufacturers supply their transducers, speed and temperature sensors as separate units. Obviously, for the temperature and speed senders to operate, they must also be in the water, and a transom mount is the logical place to mount the transducer, particularly on a small boat.

The first job is to assemble the transducer's mounting bracket. This may differ from brand to brand and even from model to model, but today almost all sounder manufacturers use transducers from the Airmar Company. The instruction sheet supplied with these transducers is excellent and you should have little trouble in following the directions. After the transducer and mounting bracket are assembled, the mounting position on the transom is selected—this is the important part of the job.

If the boat is tiller steered then it makes little difference which side of the transom the transducer is mounted, in fact the location of the display unit will probably dictate the side of the transom that you mount the transducer. However, if the boat has forward controls, the transducer should always be mounted on the port side and the transducer cable run up on the port side of the boat, away from the motor's electrical wiring, which normally is routed along the starboard side of the hull to the helm. This is very important because if the motor and transducer cables are run together, interference from the high voltage spikes present in the motor circuit will be induced into the transducer cable and show up on the sounder screen as noise, which in severe cases can blank out the picture. Another important point is never to shorten the transducer cable under any circumstances. This cable is part of the transducer's tuned circuit and shortening it will upset the tuning, resulting in a loss of power and overall performance.

The secret in getting good transducer performance, particularly at speed, is to have the transducer always in 'clean' water. That is a smooth, even, undisturbed flow of water across the face of the transducer, known as a laminar flow. (Fig 71) The old adage of a picture being worth a thousand words, is very true when discussing transducer placement, so take careful note of the drawings, they will help you grasp the idea of correct positioning.

(Fig 71) Water flow across the face of transducer

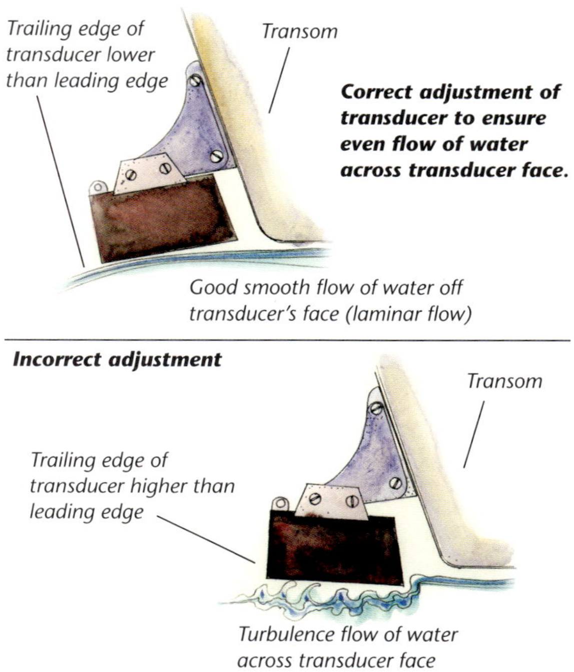

Illustrations: Trevor Hawkins

Site the transducer about 150 mm from the motor leg, this measurement is not critical, but do not put the transducer too far out from the centre of the hull. A transducer positioned out towards the chine line will lift out of the water as the boat rolls in a seaway, causing drastic interruptions to the signal and produce a picture that keeps breaking up. If the hull is fibreglass it will probably have planing strakes running along the bottom to the transom. If it is possible to position the transducer on one of these strakes, do so, even if it means moving the transducer closer, or further away from the centre line—that is within reason. If you do decide to use a planing strake, keep the transducer in a little from the outside edge, or step, of the strake as this is an area of turbulence. The transducer should be about 2 to 3 mm below the bottom of the boat.

If your hull is aluminium it will have corrugations along the bottom, unless it is a plate hull. Again, position the transducer about 150 mm out from the motor, but make sure it is in between the corrugations. Since these corrugations tend to trap air bubbles, which run along the bottom of the hull, the transducer should be a little lower than on a fibreglass boat to get the transducer's face below these bubbles, 5 to 6 mm below the hull is about right. For a plate hull, position the transducer as you would on a fibreglass boat. (Fig 72)

Some manufacturers, notably Lowrance and Eagle, supply skimmer type transducers. The position on the boat is basically the same for all types but the skimmers are fitted lower on the transom and do not require angling down at the rear because their shape promotes a laminar flow of water over the face. The transducers have a moulded line or groove around the middle and this line should be parallel with the bottom of the boat and about 20 to 25 mm below the hull line. (Fig 73)

POSITIONING TRANSDUCER ON FIBREGLASS HULL

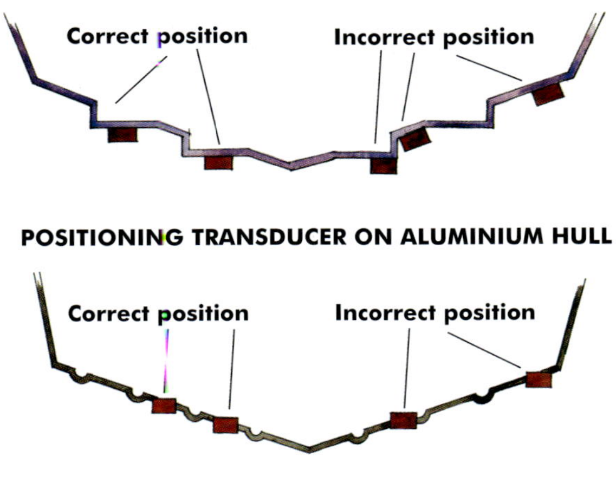

(Fig 72) Positioning transducers

SKIMMER TYPE TRANSDUCER

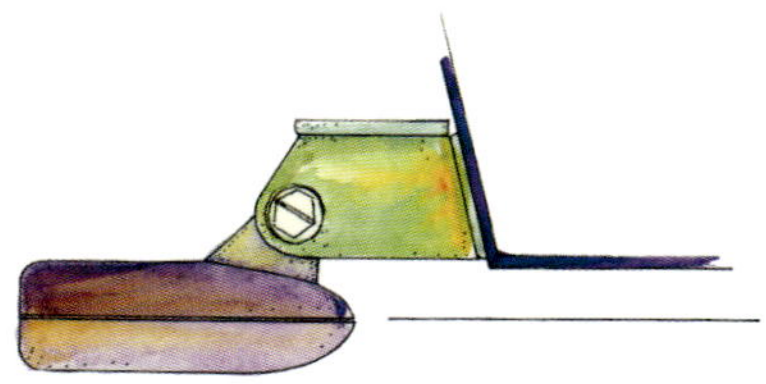

(Fig 73) Skimmer type transducer

TRANSOM MOUNT TRANSDUCER

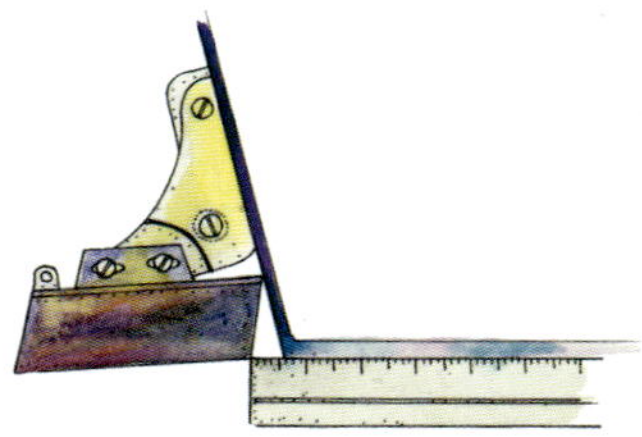

(Fig 74) Transom mount transducer

Place a steel rule or straight edge along the bottom of the boat to judge the approximate position of the transducer and mark the position of the mounting holes on the hull. The bracket will have elongated holes for future adjustments, make the hole position at the bottom of each slot as if later adjustment is needed it will always be to lower the transducer deeper into the water. By selecting the bottom of the adjustment slot it allows for maximum corrections. (Fig 74)

Take the bracket away and drill the holes for the mounting screws. These will probably be stainless steel self tapers which is fine in fibreglass and the heavier aluminium. If the transducer is being fitted to a smaller aluminium hull with lighter material, a block of wood should be fitted to the inside of the hull to take the screws and reinforce the transom at this point. Screw the transducer on making sure to seal the holes with Silastic or a similar product.

Again, hold a steel rule along the bottom of the hull and view the transducer from the side. Adjust the angle as in the drawing so as to have the back of the transducer slightly lower than the leading edge. This is a critical adjustment. If this angle is reversed, so that the leading edge is lower than the back of the transducer, there will be a great deal of turbulence as soon as the boat moves through the water and the picture will be lost even at slow speeds. Some installation instructions recommend no angle at all, however while this will work, there is no room for error and even a very small backward angle will give trouble, so I always prefer to be safe and always have a slightly positive angle. Once this is correct, tighten all of the adjustment screws.

Most of transducer mounts incorporate a 'kick-up' bracket that enables the transducer to swing up if struck by a foreign object when the boat is travelling at speed. This is usually a couple of clips that engage in the side mounting plates and are held in engagement by spring tension. This tension should be adjusted at this stage so that it takes a fairly powerful jerk to disengage the transducer. During the on-the-water setting up, this adjustment will be fine tuned to ensure the transducer will remain down when the boat is travelling at top speed, yet still disengage if any additional pressure is placed on it by striking something in the water or hitting the transducer when launching or retrieving the boat.

If the transducer incorporates a speed and distance paddle wheel this will be mounted on the rear of the transducer, usually simply clipped in. If a foreign object strikes the paddle wheel, the wheel will come out of the clips before any damage is done to the transducer. Since the wheel is only connected to the transducer by clips, the wheel will be lost. Replacement paddle wheels are freely available, however by attaching the wheel to the transducer or the transom by a loop of nylon fishing line, the wheel will be retained and most times can be re-fitted to the transducer.

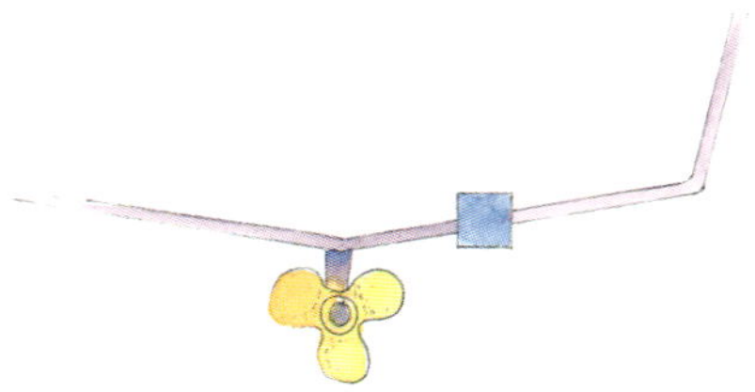

Single screw inboard

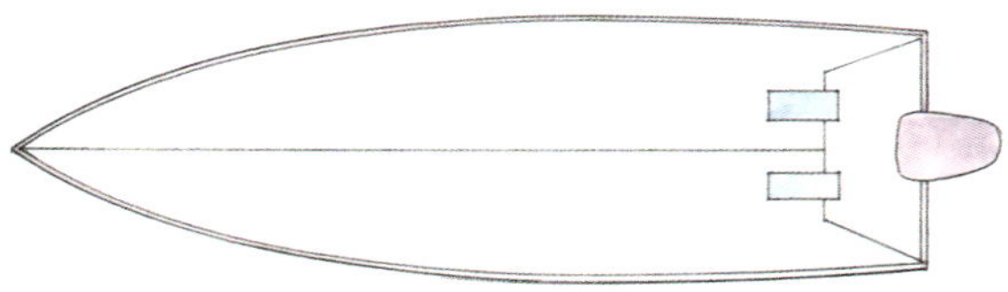

Outbard runabout

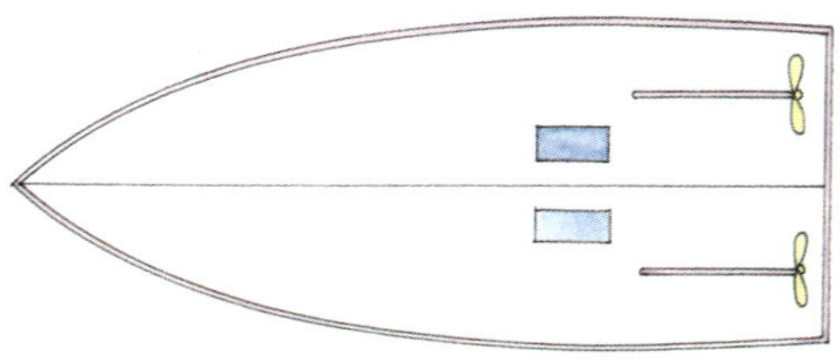

Twin screw inboard

(Fig 75)
Positions for through-hull transducers for inboard powered vessels
These are generally the best locations to install a through-hull transducer in boats with inboard motors, for the various motor configurations.

Through-hull transducers

Fitting a transducer to a boat equipped with inboard motor requires the in-hull transducer be fitted forward of the propeller (or propellers) to avoid the turbulence created by the prop.

This is probably the best method of transducer installation in this type of boat as the transducer is in clean, turbulence free water and reasonably well protected from damage. While this type of installation requires considerably more work than a transom fitting, it is not very difficult a project and a reasonably competent handyman should have no problems tackling it. Through-hull transducer is made in bronze (the most common), plastic and occasionally stainless steel. Bronze transducers are fitted to fibreglass and wooded hulls, plastic transducers are fitted to metal hulls, particularly aluminium, and stainless steel can also be used in aluminium hulls.

The face of the transducer should be parallel to the water surface when the boat is underway, and most boats will have some deadrise, therefore a fairing block of some kind will need to be fitted between the transducer and the hull to ensure the transducer is correctly orientated.

Selecting the correct location for the transducer is important and since a hole must be cut through the hull, it pays to check carefully that the location is correct, and then check again before starting to cut. Firstly, the transducer must be ahead of the propeller, but not so far forward the transducer will be lifted clear of the water when the boat is running hard on the plane or in rough sea conditions. Usually the best locations are in the last third of the hull. (Fig 75)

If the boat is to be trailed, winch the boat off and on the trailer, carefully observing where the trailer rollers bear on the hull during the loading and unloading process. Obviously these places must be avoided for locating the transducer.

Once an approximate position has been located, check there are no fittings on the hull, such as water inlets or outlets, or strakes or irregularities etc, that are forward of the selected location, which may cause turbulence to flow back over the transducer. Mark the location on the hull and then by careful—very careful—measurement, determine the location on the inner hull to make sure there are no obstructions. When you are satisfied, drill a small, 3 mm (1/8 inch), pilot hole and then check, both inside and outside the hull that this hole is in the right position. If the hole is not in the correct position, it is much easier to repair a small hole than a large one.

If this pilot hole is right then go ahead and cut the hole to fit the stem on the transducer from outside of the hull using the right size drill bit or hole saw. Be sure to hold the drill plumb so the hole will be perpendicular to the water's surface. Refer to the illustrations for an understanding of the transducer's position and fairing blocks. (Fig 76)

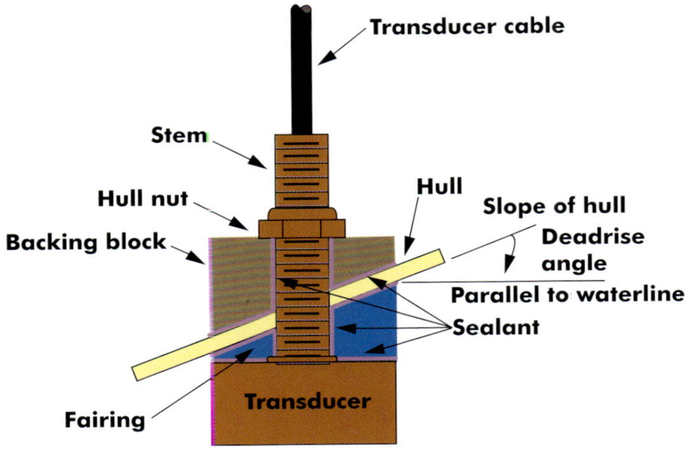

(Fig 76) Cross section of through-hull installation
A cross section views of a through-hull transducer illustrating the correct location of the parts. Refer to the text for full details of the fitting.

Traditionally fairing blocks were made from wood, however this requires considerable skill and today plastic fairings are available from the transducer manufacturers to suit most hulls, which greatly simplifies the job. (Fig 77) A backing block, usually wood, is required inside the hull to provide a level surface for the large hull nut to seat against. This backing block must be made to match the deadrise of the hull.

Once all the blocks have been made, clean the outside and inside of the hull and thread the cable through the blocks, hull and the hull nut. Apply a good coat of silicone marine sealant to both the inside and outside of the hull and the fairing blocks then fit the transducer. There is generally an arrow on the transducer housing to indicate the front of the transducer, it is important the front of the transducer faces the bow of the boat, particularly if the transducer has an integral paddle wheel for speed and distance readings. Once all is correctly aligned, firmly tighten the backing nut which should squeeze the sealant out all around the fairing blocks, wipe this excess off on the outside to ensure a smooth, uninterrupted water flow over the face of the transducer.

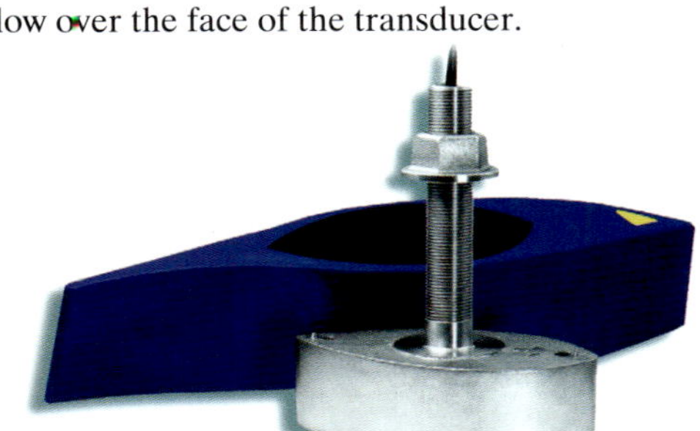

(Fig 77) Transducer fairing
A custom made fairing from Airmar to fit their range of through-hull transducers. These fairings are cut to the correct deadrise angle of the hull when fitted to give a smooth flow of water around and over the transducer for high speed operation.

Allow several hours for the sealant to cure and then place the boat in the water and check for leaks. If the boat is to be moored, this is doubly important as even a very small leak can have disastrous consequences. After several hours with the boat in the water check again for any weeps. If there is a leak then the boat will have to be removed from the water and the sealing process repeated.

If the boat is to be left in the water, particularly salt water, for any length of time, anti-fouling paint should be applied to the transducer and the fairings. It is recommended that only a water based paint be used, as solvents used in other paints may attack and break down plastics.

In-hull transducer

Using this method the transducer is glued to the hull of the boat and the sounder pluses are 'fired' through the hull. In-hull transducer mounting is only suitable for solid fibreglass hulls. Balsa or foam cored hulls are not suitable. The advantages of this method is the transducer is inside the hull and protected from knocks and bumps however some loss of signal is inevitable due to a percentage of the acoustic energy being adsorbed by the fibreglass hull. It is important the hull area chosen to mount the transducer is solid fibreglass and contains no foam, or wood sandwiched between the layers of glass.

The best location is in the stern area of the boat, which is in contact with the water at all times, even when the boat is travelling at speed. Once the general location is selected a few simple, on-water tests will confirm the best spot to mount the transducer.

If soundings are required from deep water (80 metres or more) then the testing should be carried out in this depth of water, if at all possible. If this is not feasible then do the testing in a depth of at least 30 metres (100 feet). Connect the transducer to the sounder and hold the transducer in the water beside the boat, it may be necessary to attach the transducer to a pole to comfortably reach the water. Never hold the transducer by the cable or put any strain on the cable as this could damage the transducer. Make sure the face of the transducer is parallel to the water surface and the transducer is fully submerged. Adjust the sounder to display a good bottom reading and note the control settings and the width of the bottom display.

With the boat in the same location, use one of two methods to check the actual location for the transducer. If the transducer is to be mounted in the stern area and the deadrise is not too great, make sure the bottom of the hull in this area is reasonably clean and put enough water into the bilge to cover the face of the transducer when it is located in the area. Compare the sounders reading with the first reading, taking note of the gain settings needed to obtain a display similar to the first reading, and the thickness and intensity of the bottom reading. Move the transducer around to obtain the best reading. As mentioned earlier, some loss of signal is to be expected, it is up to the operator to decide if this loss is acceptable.

The second method of testing can be carried out in just about any area of the boat and degree of deadrise. Place the transducer in a thin plastic bag, partially fill the bag with water and tightly seal the bag around the cable using cable ties or something similar. Wet the area of the hull and place the bag in good contact with the hull, keeping the transducer's face parallel to the water. Now compare the soundings as before. (Fig 78) once a satisfactory location has been selected, by either method, a final check should be made with the boat underway, if all is OK then proceed to mount the transducer.

If the deadrise is 10 degrees or less than the transducer may be mounted direct on the hull using epoxy resin. Make sure the hull is clean and dry and give it a light sanding. Check that the face of the transducer is clean and dry and then coat both surfaces with the epoxy resin and press firmly together, ensuring there are no bubbles trapped between. Do not disturb until the epoxy has set and hardened.

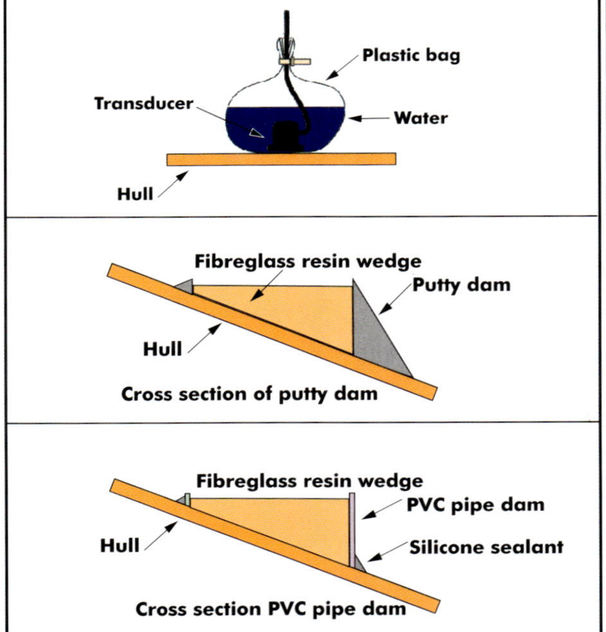

(Fig 78) Testing hull for suitability of in-hull transducer
This is an illustration of a method for testing the inside a hull for suitable areas to install an in-hull transducer. Also illustrated is a method of constructing compensating wedges for hulls with greater than ten degrees of deadrise. A simple method is to make a small 'dam' of putty and fill it with fibreglass resin. A dam may also be made by cutting a small section of PVC pipe at the same angle as the deadrise and securing it to the cleaned section of the hull using an adhesive such as silicone. Take particular care to ensure there are no bubbles in the mixture. When this has set hard the transducer is glued to the fibreglass compensating wedge using epoxy.

If the deadrise is greater than 10 degrees then a compensating wedge will have to be constructed of acoustic transparent material. See (Fig 78) for full details.

Transducer 'eye'

Since the in-hull installation is only suitable for fibreglass hulls there is a variation on this method that can be used to mount an in-hull transducer in other types of hulls. (Fig 79) This is particularly suitable for small aluminium boats, which are to be carried on vehicle roofs or regularly dragged up onto beaches, as using this mounting method the transducer is totally protected inside the hull, unlike transom mounts. Select the location for the transducer and, using a hole saw, cut a 50 mm (2 inch) hole in the hull. If the hull has pressed corrugations, select an area between these corrugations. Bolt or pop rivet a piece of fibreglass over the hole with plenty of overlap and seal with sealant. Small off-cuts of fibreglass are available at shipwright's shops that fitout boats. It only needs to be about 5 mm (1/4 inch) or so thick. The transducer is then mounted on this fibreglass 'eye'. If the deadrise is greater than ten degrees then an acoustic transparent wedge will need to be fitted as outlined in the in-hull section.

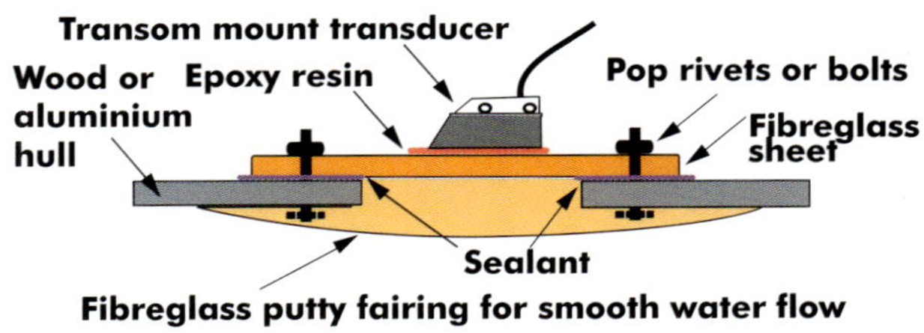

(Fig 79) Transducer eye
A technique for installing an in-hull transducer in aluminium or plywood hulls. See the text for a full explanation of this method.

Fitting the display unit

The next step is to select the actual position of the display unit. This location should be such that it offers a clear view to the helmsman but does not obstruct his view and the sounder controls should be in easy reach of the operator. On smaller boats with tiller steering, it is not unusual for the boat to be steered from the stern but fishing is carried out from a different location in the boat. This is particularly so if an electric outboard is used. In these circumstances, a second location for the sounder display is desirable. A number of suppliers offer additional mounting brackets, many of them quick connect and disconnect variety for just this type of setup. (Fig 80)

(Fig 80) Snap type sounder mounting
The Humminbird type of quick mount makes locating the sounder display in several positions on the boat a simple proposition. These mounts are standard on just about all Humminbird's sounders—they are both robust and extremely reliable.

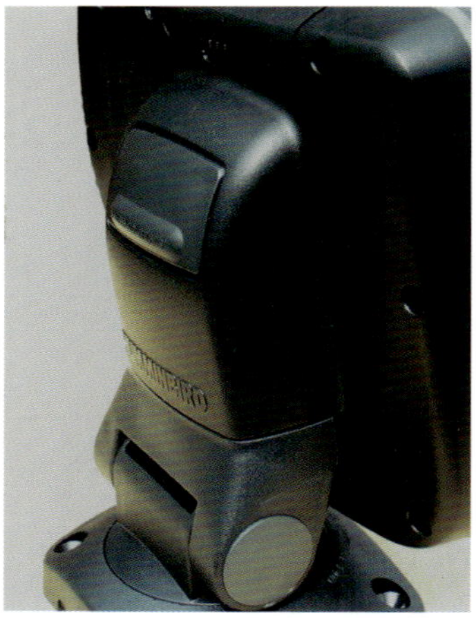

RAM brackets offer a convenient method of mounting the display unit, particularly when space is at a premium. They are also an excellent means of mounting sounders in small boats that do not have a dashboard. (Fig 81 and Fig 82)

Since all transducers are supplied with around 6 metres of transducer cable, which cannot be shortened, having enough cable is seldom an issue. The main point to be aware of is to make sure any loose cable is properly stowed away, eliminating the chance of it being damaged by dropping something on it, standing on it or cutting it.

(Fig 81)

(Fig 82)

(Fig 81) & (Fig 82) Ram type mounting
The RAM mounting system is an ideal system for mounting sounders and other equipment, particularly where dashboard space is limited or is non-existent as it often is in open boats. Typical of this kind of installation is the picture of the sounder and handheld GPS fitted to the gunwales of a Quintrex Hornet open runabout. The mounts feature a double ball and socket mounting, making fitting to almost any surface a simple exercise. The system also ideal when a unit needs to be quickly fitted in several different locations in the boat.

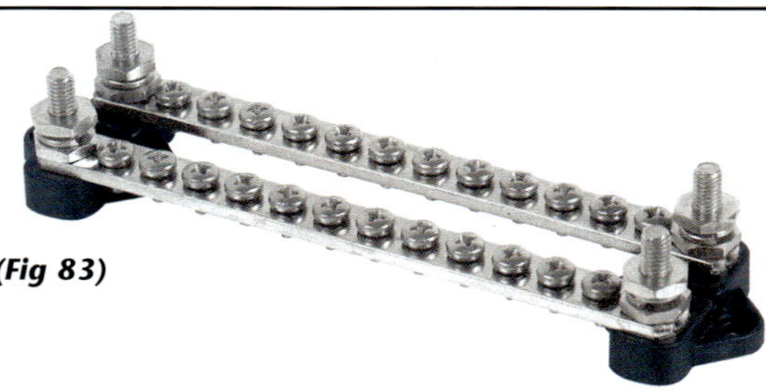

(Fig 83)

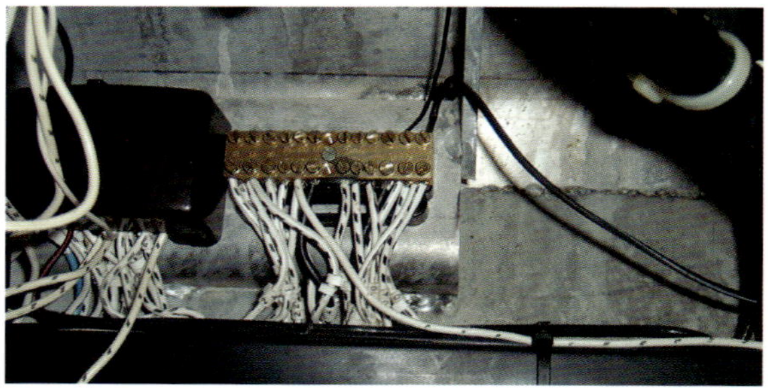

(Fig 84)

(Fig 83) & (Fig 84) Neutral link buss bars
Buss bars are used to terminate wiring, usually the negative or neutral connects. Neutral link connecting blocks, as used in domestic household switchboards, make satisfactory terminal blocks (Fig. 83), or the custom designed BEP buss bars (Fig. 84) make for a very neat installation. Covers are available and should be fitted, particularly if the back of the panel is open to salt air, such as behind dashboards etc. Also, at the time of installation it is worth the effort to fit number identification tags to the wiring as it saves a lot of trouble if faultfinding is needed in the future.

Now route the transducer cable neatly up the transom and secure with a couple of clips so there is no movement to cause chafing when the boat is underway. Run the cable up to the position selected for mounting the display unit. Again, secure with plenty of ties to prevent any chance of the cable rubbing against the hull. Cable ties make this a simple job provided the boat manufacturer has included brackets under the gunwales for attaching cables. If not, brackets will need to be fitted to firmly support the cable. Brackets to support the cables need not be all that sophisticated, 50 mm sections of plastic pipe, such as PVC waste pipe about 30 to 50 mm in diameter glued beneath the gunwales using a strong adhesive such as Sikaflex, is a simple and efficient method to support the cables.

Connect the power cable to the battery power supply. A good method is to run earth and positive cables direct from the boat's battery to positive and negative buss bars behind the dashboard. (Fig 83 and Fig 84) All of the electrical and electronic equipment is then connected to these buss bars. The cables used to connect the buss bars to the battery should be robust enough to ensure there is no appreciable voltage drop when all the electric equipment is operating. Low voltage can adversely affect the sounder's performance, particularly when working in deep water. The ideal set-up is to have a dedicated battery, isolated from the motor's starting battery to supply power to all the boat's electronic equipment. A battery that is used only for the boat's electronics and is electrically isolated from the motor starting battery will prevent 'high voltage spikes' from possibly damaging some items of electronics—GPS in particular. (Fig 85) The circuit diagram illustrates a method of charging the auxiliary battery from the boat's motor charging circuit, but automatically disconnecting the auxiliary battery from the circuit when starting the motor by the use of a voltage sensitive relay.

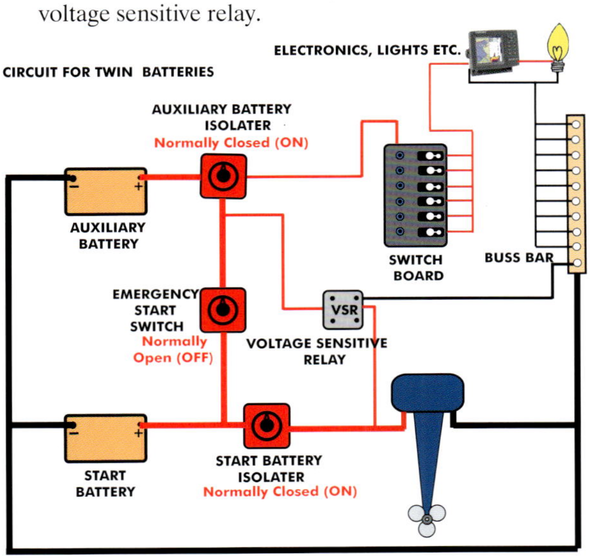

(Fig 85) Circuit for dual batteries
This is a circuit that uses a voltage sensitive relay to ensure the auxiliary battery, which supplies power to the electronics, is isolated from the motor starting battery when the engine is started, to prevent spikes from damaging the electronic components. The relay also detects when the starting battery has reached full charge and then directs the charging current from the motor's alternator to the auxiliary battery.

It is not strictly necessary to power the sounder through an on/off switch as all units have a dedicated switch that is usually part of the sensitivity control. It is, however, important to protect the sounder with a fuse. An in-line fuse will have been supplied with the sounder, or a separate fuse may be used, provided the fuse is of the correct rating. A fuse can prevent a minor problem becoming a catastrophic event. If at all possible it is desirable to fit the fuses behind the dashboard to protect them from weather and spray. All fuses are prone to corrosion and should be checked regularly to ensure a good power supply to the sounder.

However, fuses are, unfortunately, a necessary evil as they are quite prone to corrosion, even when protected from water, the presence of salt air is sufficient to corrode the fuse's end caps, which are lightly plated steel, in a surprisingly short time. A viable alternative is circuit breakers, particularly those designed specifically for marine applications. While circuit breakers are more expensive than fuses they offer many advantages. Unlike fuses, a circuit breaker does not 'blow' but will 'trip' in the advent of an overload, and once the fault is repaired, they can be reset. The circuit breaker is also a switch.

Circuit breakers and switches can be mounted on custom boards or there is a vast range of 'off the shelf' boards to suit any installation. These switch boards are supplied with circuit breakers and legends and come virtually ready to install. (Fig 86 and Fig 87)

Connect the transducer cable to the unit. If the sounder has been flush mounted into the dashboard this is a simple task. However, if the sounder has been mounted on top of the dash, or console etc, using the gimbal bracket supplied, then the power and transducer cables will need to be routed through a hole in the mounting surface. This hole will need to be large enough to allow the transducer plug to pass through and the hole should be filled with silicone and tidied up by covering with a clam shell, which is a dress cover available at boat chandlers. A clam shell may also be used to cover the transducer cable hole on the transom. Before securing the cables, check that sufficient length has been left in the cables to enable the sounder to be fitted and removed from its bracket without straining the cables.

(Fig 86)

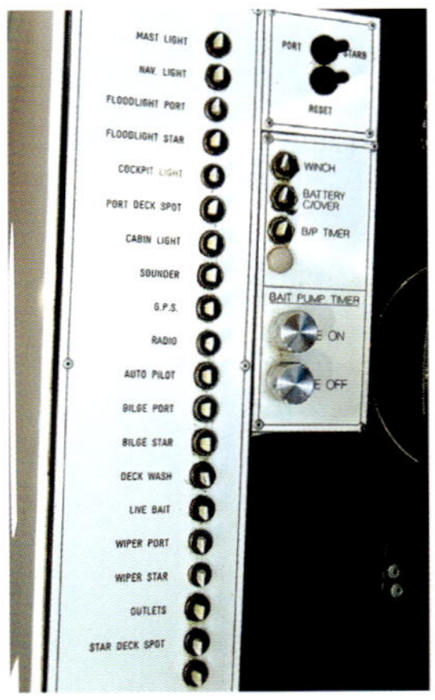

(Fig 87)

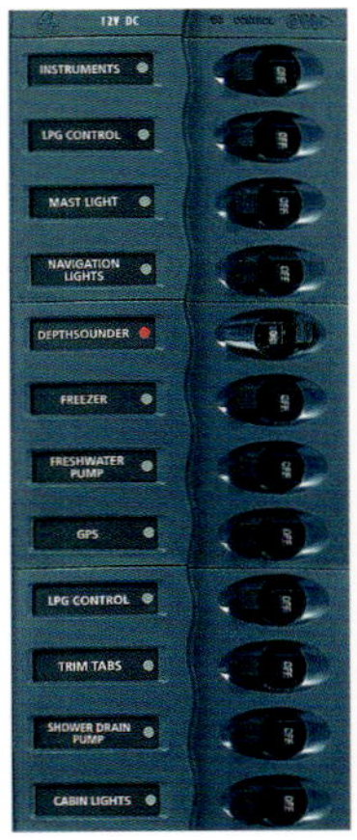

(Fig 86) & (Fig 87) Switch boards
Circuit breakers and switches may be mounted on custom made boards, constructed from engraved panels (Fig. 85), or ready-made boards may be purchased. BEP has a large range of boards and can supply heavy duty battery switches and voltage sensitive relays.

On-water testing and final tuning

The following instructions refer in the main to transom mount transducers but, with the exception of adjusting the transducer, they apply equally to through-hull and in-hull transducers. It is worthwhile noting there is seldom a problem with either of these mounting systems, apart from induced electrical noise, however even this fault is rare, particularly if care has been taken in selecting the transducer's cables route to the display unit.

The first item to check after installation is completed is the power supply and the sounder itself. This merely consists of connecting the power cable to the unit and checking it will turn on and off, that the display comes up and the controls all operate. If the unit has a simulator mode (today almost all sounders are fitted with this facility) switch over to this and have a play with the controls to familiarise yourself with the basic operation of the sounder. At this time a few extra minutes spent studying the owner's manual and instruction book is time well spent.

Once the boat is launched, move out into a reasonable depth (over five metres) and turn the sounder on. With the boat stationary, select the sounder's manual operating mode and adjust the range to position the bottom in the lower third of the screen and turn the gain (or sensitivity) up until the screen starts to show 'speckles' and then just back-off until the interference clears up. It may be worth noting at this point that many sounders automatically power-up in the 'auto' mode, so make sure you are in the manual mode for these tests. If your boat is outboard powered, there is usually no problem in having the motor running in idle during this set up stage, however if your boat has an inboard/outboard leg you may have to turn the motor off. The reason for this is outboard motors, when idling, expel most of the exhaust gases through a relief port on the rear of the motor above water level, the majority of the exhaust only passes out through the prop when the boat is underway. However, with an inboard/outboard a lot of the exhaust goes into the water, even at idle and if these bubble up around the transducer the signal will be lost or badly degraded and give erroneous readings, which may indicate faults in the installation that in reality do not exist.

Once the display is adjusted correctly, put the motor into gear and move off. Slowly increase the speed while watching the display. (At this point it is an advantage to have crew who can take over running the boat while you concentrate on the sounder display). If all is well the picture should remain clean and steady as the boat picks up speed and it should stay that way until at least about 20 knots, probably much higher if the water is calm.

If you have followed the installation instructions, the odds are very much in your favour that the sounding will be right first time. Over the last 25 years I have fitted many hundreds of sounders and the vast majority, about 99 per cent, were right the first time, and with the remaining 1 per cent, the problem was usually rectified by lowering the transducer.

When conducting the initial tests on your sounder, if the screen becomes cluttered with interference even at low speeds, there are a number of tests to carry out to pinpoint the cause of problem. These tests are a series of elimination steps, and should be carried out in the order listed so as to ensure one fault is not masking another. Firstly, stop the boat and rev the motor in neutral using the hand throttle. If the picture breaks up when the boat is stationary then the fault is noise induced from the motor and it may be necessary to run a separate power supply direct from the battery, or even to fit a dedicated battery to supply power only to the electronics. However, while it is worth checking, it is very unlikely this will be the problem, as modern sounders are very well protected from this type of external interference. If you have an inboard/outboard do this test with the boat moving slowly forward so as to drift the exhaust bubbles away from the transducer.

If the display is fine after the rev test, then engage forward gear and note when the picture begins to deteriorate. If you loose the picture at a comparative low speed, return to the ramp and check that the transducer has not moved from its original setting. Particularly check that the back of the transducer is still lower than the front. If this all checks out fine, lower the whole transducer about 6 to 10 mm, and repeat the performance test of the sounder. The chances are all will be well.

In the rare incidences that this does not fix the problem, then it may be necessary to reposition the transducer. Before this is undertaken it is essential to select a new location on the transom that has an uninterrupted flow of water. To do this have a crew member drive the boat at planing speed while you observe the water coming away from the transom. The transducer must be positioned in the smoothest flow of water, with the face of the transducer skimming just below the surface. If possible select the location within the zone of between 150 and 250 mm from the motor leg. But I must stress it is very unlikely you will need to even adjust the transducer.

When you have a good clean picture at planing speed, you know your unit is working as it should, however do not expect to be able to get this type of display under all conditions. If the water is choppy, bubbles of air are forced beneath the boat by the waves, causing the picture to break-up. It may be necessary to come off the plane to get a decent picture. Also, the deeper the water the more difficult it is to get clean pictures, particularly in choppy conditions.

It is worth considering just what speed is appropriate. I have found if you are just running the sounder as you travel from one fishing location to another in the hope you may unexpectedly run across a new spot, then 15 knots is about the top practical speed. Anything higher and you have your hands full handling the boat and are not able to properly watch the sounder. When you are close to your mark, 7 to 8 knots is tops, and when you have located the spot, and are looking for fish and a location to anchor, 3 to 5 knots is plenty.

Chapter ten

Maintenance

With the installation and testing of your new sounder complete, the next step is to go out and catch a few fish, however here are a few final words on maintenance of your new pride and joy. Fortunately, keeping a sounder installation in good working order requires very little time or effort and consists mainly on checking for faults before they develop. Boats and water is a pretty tough environment, particularly when electric current is concerned. Corrosion will set in on electrical contacts in an amazingly short time, and it is for this reason all electrical joints should be soldered wherever possible, however there are some locations when this is not practical, such as connecting plugs, sockets and fuses.

When voltage and moisture are present together, some electrical current will flow between conductors. A conductor in this context is any metal connected to the power source such as wiring, conductors (pins) in plugs and sockets etc. Typically this current flow will be small, however over time it will cause electrolysis resulting in corrosion in one or both of the terminals, and in severe cases will actually eat away the conductors, particularly those small pins and sockets used as connecting plugs on many sounders. (Fig 88)

The simplest and most obvious way to prevent this type of deterioration is to remove the power source whenever the equipment is not being used, and the easiest method is to install a battery isolating switch in the battery circuit. An added bonus if your hull is aluminium, is a marked reduction of corrosion in the hull. (Fig 89)

If your rig is a trailer boat with a transom mounted transducer, occasionally give the face of the transducer a good wash with warm soapy water. The reason for this is that when the boat is being trailered, road grime and oil can build up on the transducer's face, which can be detrimental to the unit's performance. Mild detergent can be used to wash the transducer's face but steer clear of any harsh detergents that may break down the plastic material on the transducer.

(Fig 88) Corroded plugs
This is an example of the damage that can be caused to electrical equipment that is left connected to a battery supply for long period in a salt atmosphere. Salt is deposited on the surface of the plug and a minute amount of current flows between the positive and negative pins causing severe corrosion.

(Fig 89) Battery switches
To prevent corrosively damaging currents within the boat's wiring and electrical equipment, all batteries within the boat should be isolated, when the boat is not in use, by means of marine battery switches.

If the boat is carried on roof racks (Fig 90) and the transducer is removed each time the boat is used, remember to take care to ensure the transducer is adjusted correctly, as this is the most crucial adjustment for good performance. This also applies if you swing the transducer, on its bracket, up clear of obstructions for loading onto a car top or beach the boat. When used in this way, and the transducer is moved on a regular basis, the retaining bolt tends to be not as tight as when the installation is a fixed one. In these cases the transducer may come out of alignment and needs regular checking

If the transducer is a through-hull installation or a transom mount on a boat that is moored or kept in a marina, the transducer should be given a coat of anti-fouling paint at regular intervals. The time between coats will vary with the location, but once every 12 months is about normal. If you notice a marked loss of performance, particularly sensitivity, the transducer's face should be checked for marine growth. If the through-hull transducer incorporates a paddle wheel for speed and distance readings, this should be removed when moored to prevent marine growth, particularly shells, from fouling the paddle wheel.

The sounder display unit can be given a coat of a silicone protective spray such as Armor All, which not only keeps the sounder looking good but provides a silicone coating that makes the removal of dust and water marks a breeze.

(Fig 90) Transporting boats
Many boats are transported on the roof racks of vehicles and this usually means the transducer is removed from the boat before loading. When refitting the transducer ensure the angle of the transducer is correct, as even a small degree of misalignment can cause poor sounding results. For full details on the correct angle see the section on sounder installation.

Part two
The GPS

Chapter eleven

History & Basic Principles

(Fig 1) GPS satellite constellation

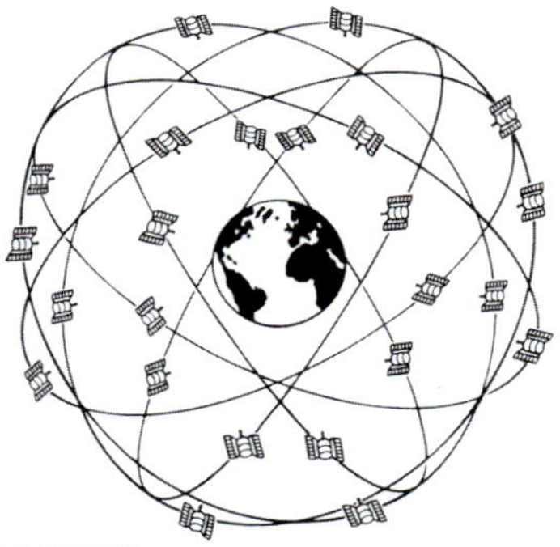

THE SATELLITES

The Global Positioning System became fully operational in the early 1990's, although partial coverage was provided for some years before (the first satellite was launched in February 1989 and the most recent 25 September 2005.) The system now consists of 30 satellites in a high polar orbit, some 20,200 kilometres above the earth (fig 1). The orbit design was developed to guarantee that at least four satellites are always in view at every point on the earth's surface twenty-four hours a day. In many instances, however, as many as twelve or thirteen satellites will be visible to the earth based user. Each satellite in the constellation orbits the earth twice a day. The satellites continually transmit a unique coded sequence, which allows identification of the satellite, precise time correction signals, as well as almanac data for all the satellites in the constellation.

GPS RECEIVERS

The GPS receiver measures the time of arrival of each signal and then calculates the range (distance) of each satellite. Once the range of the satellites is known, the position of the receiver can be determined by triangulation. If it were possible to measure 'true satellite ranges' directly it would only be necessary to track data from two satellites to obtain your latitude and longitude. The range measurement depends on accurately measuring the time taken for the radio signal, which is travelling at the speed of light, to reach the receiver. Unfortunately these transmissions are affected by the ionosphere as well as by timing errors in the receiver's own internal clock, so a minimum of three satellites is required to cancel out these errors to obtain an initial fix.

GPS TIME

Accurate time is critical to the operation of GPS and to this end each satellite has four atomic clocks on board and the performance of these clocks is regularly monitored and adjusted by earth stations. As you would appreciate, time is of prime importance in GPS and the satellites refer to UTC (Universal Time Coordinates) time, which for all practical purposes is the same as GMT (Greenwich Mean Time). (For the purest, UTC is about 5 seconds ahead of GMT.) Each satellite's time is checked and corrected on a weekly basis by the earth stations

SATELLITE CODES AND SELECTIVE AVAILABILITY

The satellites transmit on two frequencies, 1575.42 MHz and 1227.60 MHz, which are known as the 'L-band' and a second band L2C. Each signal has sequence codes superimposed on the carrier frequency by modulation.

These codes are a Precision Code (P) and a Course Acquisition Code (C/A). The P code is reserved for the military and the C/A code for civilian use. It was originally intended that the P code would be considerably more accurate than the C/A code, yet when implemented, the difference was not as significant as the system designers had expected. To deny the unexpected accuracy of the system to anyone other than the United States military and friendly allies, a deliberate degrading of the system was introduced in early 1991.

This intended error was called Selective Availability (S/A), also know as dithering of the signal, which reduced the civilian accuracy to about 100 metres. In May 2000 S/A was removed and the accuracy of the system improved to around 10–15 metres. The reasoning behind this change was improvements to the satellites now in service, which enabled the US Department of Defence to selectively degrade the accuracy of the satellite signals in any particular region. If, for instance, the US wished to render the system virtually useless in the Persian Gulf region to users of the C/A code, it only required re-programming of the satellites for that region. The rest of the world would still be able to enjoy the full accuracy of the system. Without S/A the accuracy of the system has improved dramatically, however there are a number of factors which can still effect the overall accuracy of the fix. Factors such as the satellites geometry, component tolerances, chart datum etc. The degree of accuracy that the average user can expect will be looked at later in full detail.

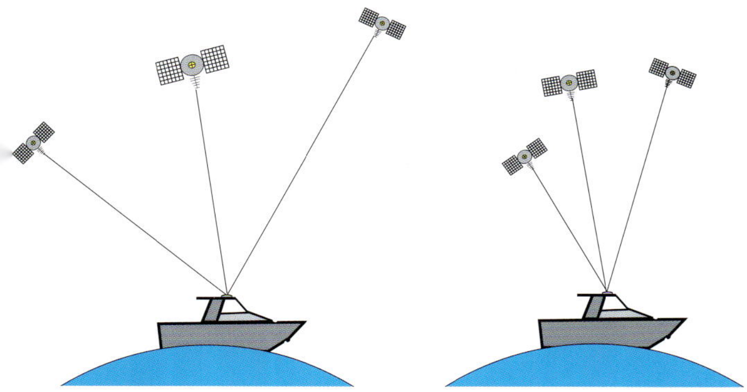

(Fig 2) HDOP
Geometry effects on accuracy which is expressed as Horizontal Dilution of Precision (HDOP), When the satellites being used for the fix are close together the HDOP figure is high and the accuracy is not as good as when the satellites are more widely separated.

DILUTION OF PRECISION

All GPS receivers are designed to select a configuration of satellites with the best geometry and by doing so provide optimum position accuracy. Thus, the greater number of satellites in view from which the GPS receiver can select the greater the accuracy. To present the user with a realistic measure of the quality of the satellite configuration a factor know as Dilution of Precision (DOP) is available on all receivers. A DOP can refer to several types of precision; the main ones are Geometric Dilution of Precision (GDOP), Positional Dilution of Precision (PDOP) and Horizontal Dilution of Precision (HDOP.)

GDOP refers to the expected precision of a three dimensional fix, that is length, breadth and height, and includes a calculation for time. PDOP is also a three dimensional factor but does not include time. HDOP is two dimensional—length and breadth—and is the factor used for marine positioning since height measurements are meaningless as the boat will always be at sea level. While some GPS receivers display all of these factors, most only show the HDOP reading. It should be remembered that HDOP is only a relative number, a multiplier in other words, which is used to calculate the error of a fix in cases when it is important to determine the probable error of any readings. The smaller the HDOP number the better the fix, a figure of three is considered very good, five is good and any readings greater than ten are going to have an appreciable effect on the accuracy of the system. Having said this it is rare today to see HDOP figures of greater than three (fig 2). Some GPS units display HDOP as a real measurement, either in feet or metres, which refers to a circle of accuracy around the boat, in other words if the display indicates an estimated error of 15 metres the true position will be within 15 metres of the boat's position.

LINE OF POSITION

When a receiver is first switched on it must obtain an initial position fix. To do this the receiver uses three satellites and, by comparison, the internal processor can determine the amount of clock error in each range calculation. The receiver subtracts the error from each range solution until the Lines of Position (LOP) intersect at one point, this then is the fix (fig 3). LOP are used in all types of navigation, for example, when you use visual marks to locate a fishing spot you are using LOP. When two objects are lined up, you know the location must lie somewhere along that line. When a second set of marks is lined up, the point where the two lines intersect is the location of your fishing spot (fig 4).

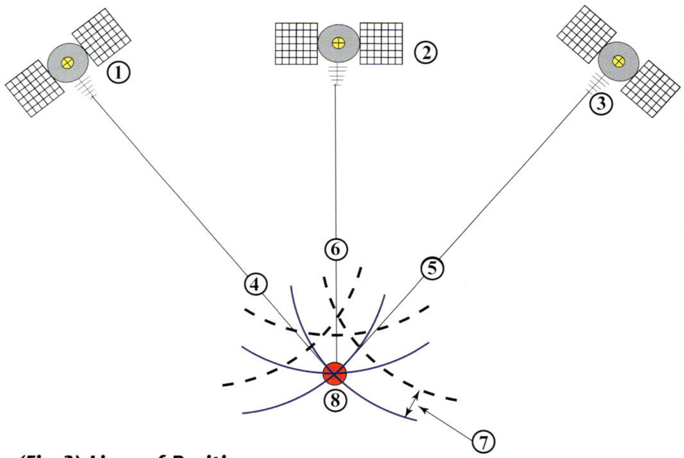

(Fig 3) Lines of Position
Each of the three satellites (1), (2) and (3) transmit a signal known as Lines of Position (LOPs), which is the term used to indicate the position of the target lays somewhere on this line. Where the three LOPs from each of the satellites (4), (5) and (6) intersect (8) this is then the correct position, which is known as a fix. The clock error (7) is corrected by the satellite's internal processor. See the text for full details.

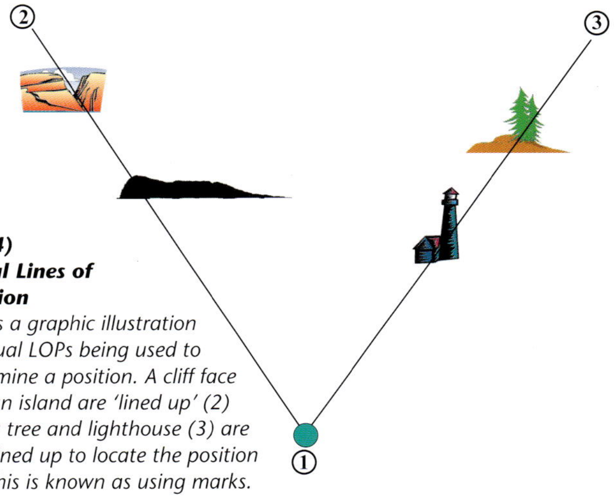

(Fig 4) Visual Lines of Position
This is a graphic illustration of visual LOPs being used to determine a position. A cliff face and an island are 'lined up' (2) and a tree and lighthouse (3) are also lined up to locate the position (1), this is known as using marks.

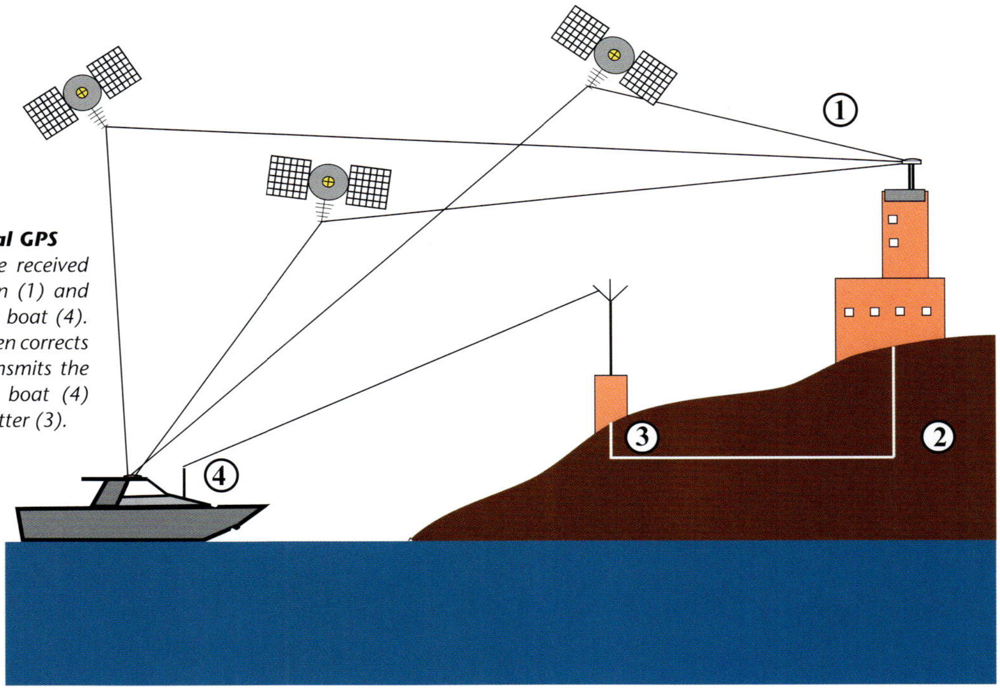

(Fig 5) Differential GPS
Satellite signals are received by the base station (1) and the receiver on the boat (4). The base station then corrects the signal and transmits the corrections to the boat (4) via a radio transmitter (3).

SATELLITE NUMBERS

All satellites are identified by numbers and these numbers are shown on the receiver's status screen, usually the number has a prefix either PRN (Pseudo-Random Number) or SVID (Space Vehicle IDentity).

DIFFERENTIAL GPS

During the years when S/A was active, a system know as Differential GPS (DGPS) was introduced. DGPS consists of a GPS receiver permanently located at a known reference point. Positional errors at the reference GPS are corrected for each satellite and these corrections are broadcast over a radio link. A DGPS set receives these radio corrections and mixes them in the standard GPS receiver greatly enhancing its accuracy (fig 5).

The limitations of such a system are the distance from the base station, radio interference and cost. Depending on the frequency of the radio data link and the distance from the base, accuracy was improved to 10 metres or less. A number of commercial (user pays) DGPS bases were set-up and use radio links in the VHF and UHF band, giving users in close proximity to the base accuracy of a couple of meters. Of main interest to the recreational user was a DGPS system established by the Commonwealth using HF frequency transmitters—this service was free to users. While VHF and UHF are almost line-of-sight frequencies, HF is long range. Initially the Government commissioned DGPS stations as a navigation aid to cover high-risk areas, such as the North West Shelf and Bass Strait oil fields, and the Great Barrier Reef passage. Later, more stations were established along the coast, particularly in areas of high commercial marine traffic.

The RF system of DGPS provided users as far away as 60 nautical miles (n miles) from the base station with accuracy's of 10–15 metres, however with the dropping of S/A by the United States Department of Defence in 2000, few recreational users found they could justify the cost of a Differential Receiver for the small increase in accuracy it offered.

FUTURE DIFFERENTIAL DEVELOPMENTS

Three systems based, rather loosely, on DGPS technology are operational overseas, however they are unlikely to be seen in Australian waters for quite some time, if ever, due to the high cost of establishing the satellites and the base stations, and their continuing costly upkeep. The North American system, called Wide Area Augmentation System (WAAS), which offers greater accuracy without many of the problems associated with DGPS—including only requiring one receiver as the correction signals are transmitted on the same frequency as the GPS signals, has less interference due to weather and has a very fast update time. The European equivalent is known as EGNOS an abbreviation for European Geostationary Navigation Overlay Service, and the MSAS, which is only available in Japan. (All of these systems use geostationary satellites as well as base stations.)

These systems were established for use in aviation navigation, particularly for landings in conditions of poor visibility at smaller airports that do not support Instrument Landing Systems (ILS systems).

While there is little likelihood of the system being established in Australia, the present GPS system generally offers accuracy of about five metres, often considerably less, which is more than adequate for most marine applications.

CHART AND MAP DATUM

Since the earth is not a true sphere, but a spheroid with the diameter at the equator greater than at the poles, to create marine charts and land maps it is necessary to have a fixed, geodetic, point on the earth's surface against which all other positions are measured. This point is called the geodetic datum. But as would be expected, there is a number of different datum in use, often changing from country to country. For the navigator it is obviously critical that the position from the GPS receiver is the same datum as that of the navigation chart, or that a GPS mark being entered was recorded using the same datum as in the GPS receiver. Most electronics charts used in chart plotters these days are WGS84 datum.

Fortunately there is a degree of uniformity appearing and the World Geodetic System of 1984 (WGS84) is fast becoming standard. Most of the Admiralty charts produced in recent years are based on WGS84 and all of the older charts printed during the last few years carry the corrections which need to be made to bring positions derived from the paper chart to agree with the GPS positions obtained if the GPS receiver's datum has been set to WGS84. For example, this is a type of notice that would appear on an Australian Chart.

Satellite – Derived Positions

Positions obtained from satellite navigation systems are referred to the WGS datum; such positions should be moved 0.09 minutes SOUTWARD and 0.06 minutes WESTWARD to agree with this chart.

Most GPS receivers have provision to change their datum to match that used on your paper chart of the area. By default, the receiver usually uses WGS84. However be aware, if the datum has been changed to suit a local chart, and another chart is used, make sure the datum of the GPS receiver is checked to see that it agrees with the new chart's datum.

If you are using a paper chart to plot your position from GPS coordinates or are transferring positions from a chart to your GPS it is VITAL that you be aware of both the datum used when the chart was drawn and the datum that the GPS is using. Similarly, you must be aware that the datum of a GPS mark that you enter into your GPS receiver must be the same as that of the GPS receiver to accurately represent the intended position. Land maps also carry notices of the datum used in their production. If there is no notice displayed on the chart or map as to the datum, use WGS84. Other than WGS84 the main datum used in Australia is Australian Geodetic Datum 1966 (AGD66) and Australian Geodetic Datum 1984 (AGD84)

An aspect of chart datum and its effect on the accuracy of the system, which is often overlooked, is transferring of coordinate data between GPS receivers. If a position fix is recorded, using the Australian AGD84 datum and this data is then transferred to a unit operating on the default WGS84 then the error will be considerable.

To correct this type of datum error a correction is applied to the coordinates to convert them to the required datum. This correction factor is obtained by setting up a GPS receiver at a fixed location and recording the coordinates and the Geodetic Datum used. Without moving the receiver, change the datum to the required one and record the coordinates. It now becomes a simple matter to calculate the correction factor. As an example, the following is the correction for my location, which is on the NSW Central Coast.

WGS84: S32 57.273 E151 37.556
AGD84: S32 57.370 E151 37.488

Correcting WGS84 to AGD84 add 0.097 to latitude and subtract 0.068 from longitude.

Correcting AGD84 to WGS84 subtract 0.097 from latitude and add 0.068 to longitude.

The difference between the two datum is about 0.1 of a nautical mile, about 200 metres.

It is important to remember the correction factor will vary according to the location, so if you change your location more than about 60 nautical miles from the location where the correction was calculated it is advisable to calculate a new factor.

Fortunately this type of error is not common as most GPS receivers have WGS84 as a default datum and few operators ever find the need to alter this configuration.

Chart datum is only of importance when transferring data to, or from, a chart or map. There are other factors, which could affect the accuracy of a position plotted from a paper chart, or plotted to a paper chart. The wise navigator will always take heed of the disclaimer published in all GPS instruction books and displayed at the start-up of the GPS receivers warning uses to exercise common prudence and navigational judgement and the device should not relied on as the only source of navigation. The rule for pilots also applies to navigators: 'There are old navigators and bold navigators, but few old, bold navigators'.

Chapter twelve
GPS Installation

CONSIDERATIONS

After reading all about the System and how it all works, now is the time to get your hands dirty and install the unit in the boat. The installation of a GPS receiver is generally a straightforward job, which should present no problems for the average handyman.

The first step is to sit down and read the installation instructions supplied with the unit, this will not only make the job easier but probably save a lot of heartache later.

LOCATING THE DISPLAY UNIT

The display unit can be fitted either as a flush mount or bracket mounting. GPS receivers that are suitable for flush mounting are generally supplied with hardware to mount the unit and a template for cutting the correct sized hole in the bulkhead. Points to be checked before starting to cut are to make sure that there is sufficient room behind the bulkhead to comfortably take the unit, that there are no obstructions, such as cabling, behind the bulkhead and the bulkhead itself is strong enough to support the display. Remember, when the boat is pounding in a sea there are considerable inertia forces placed on the mounting. Check, and then check again, that the selected location is the correct one before cutting the hole in the panel.

I have found one of the best methods for determining the right spot for both bracket and flush mounted installations is to temporarily attach the power lead to the unit and 'fire it up'. Assume your normal driving position and move the display around until all of the controls are in easy reach and you are getting a good view under all conditions. If the unit is to be bracket mounted, ensure there is enough room to swing the display through its range of adjustments. It is often advantageous to be able to swing the display so that if you are fishing from just about anywhere in the boat you can still see the display. By doing this it is possible to check—if you have anchored—that the anchor has not dragged and you have moved off the mark, or if you are drift fishing you can verify your rate and direction of drift and your current position. If all is well, temporarily mount the unit.

Bracket or gimbal mounting is much the same as for flush mounting. Check that there is room for the brackets, that the panel chosen to mount the bracket is strong enough to support the unit even in rough seas (it may be an advantage to fit a reinforcing plate under the panel if there is any doubt), and that there is space to run the cabling.

Time spent on selecting the right location is well worth the extra effort. Remember that you will use the GPS more than any other instrument on the boat, so make its location comfortable and convenient to use.

MOUNTING THE ANTENNA

While the position of the antenna is not critical there are a couple of rules to be observed. The antenna should have an uninterrupted, clear view of the whole of the sky, however glass, Perspex, fibreglass, and fabrics will not impede the signal, wood or metal will.

GPS antennas should be kept away from radio transmitter antennas. Three metres is a safe distance from high power antennas such as VHF and HF radios, but if room is tight you can creep up a little closer to the 27 MHz, which has a fairly low output. Radars are a definite no no, they radiate large amounts of radio frequency and the antenna should be kept well out of the radar beam.

On most runabouts the antenna is mounted on the foredeck, which in many ways is an ideal site. It is usually easy to find space on the deck and in this location the antenna is generally protected from the bumps and knocks that are to be expected in day to day fishing. Wiring the antenna back to the display unit is usually simple too. Many of today's antennas are compact units, which can be fitted, almost flush, straight onto the deck (fig 6). The antenna should always be mounted as near to horizontal as possibly to enable it to 'see' the sky from horizon to horizon, however when one considers the movement of the boat in a seaway, a few degrees doesn't matter. If the deck is steeply sloped it will be necessary to make up a wooden packing piece to bring the antenna back to the horizontal. Another option is to use a fully adjustable radio antenna base, which are available at most chandler supplies.

While the foredeck is a common location, there are plenty of other equally suitable sites. The antenna does not have to be mounted out in the open. If there is room it can be successfully placed on the dash provided there are no metal frames close by to mask the antenna, the windscreen will not interfere with the signal strength. The antenna can also be mounted below decks, provided the hull material is fibreglass—this is a favourite spot on yachts.

(Fig 6) Flush mounting antenna
A GPS antenna suitable for flush deck mounting.

If it is more convenient the antenna can be fitted to an overhead rod rack or targa bar (fig 7). The extra height above the water is no advantage, nor is it a disadvantage, although do not mount the antenna at the top of a high mast, the swinging about of the mast in anything of a sea will lead to errors in the received data. If you are having a rod rack or targa made up and intend to have a stub fitted at the time of manufacturer to mount the GPS antenna—be warned—the standard thread in the bases of both radio and GPS is 1 inch diameter, 14 threads to the inch. This is American thread, not the common 1 inch Whitworth thread used in Australia.

Route the antenna cable back to the display unit, making sure the cable is well secured and cannot move about and chaff on the hull. The majority of antennas are supplied with a long connecting cable, up to 6 metres to cater for remote antenna installations, but the average runabout usually only requires 1–1.5 metres. This lead may be cut; it is not a tuned circuit like a radio antenna lead. Some units have moulded plugs which cannot be opened, and even those plugs which can be serviced have small connectors, which require a certain level of skill to un-solder and re-solder the connections to shorten the lead. If you do not feel confident in attempting this job, just coil up the lead and stow it neatly in some out of the way location.

Connect the power lead from the display unit to a convenient power supply point in the boat's electrical system. LCD units draw very little current, but it still pays to ensure the connection point has a good clean supply. Make sure you fit the fuse supplied with the unit and if the GPS has a ferrite suppression block supplied, also fit this around the power cable.

Attach the antenna cable to the unit and switch it on, if everything checks out okay install the display permanently and tidy up the cables.

VOLTAGE SPIKES

All electronic equipment is subjected to voltage spikes and fluctuations in the boat's power supply, but a GPS is particularly prone to problems from this type of interference. These spikes can create serious problems in electronic equipment, although they can usually be overcome with a little care, planning and knowledge.

Spikes are spurious fluctuations in the power supply from the battery, generated by other equipment operating from the same supply at the same time. Spikes can take two forms, high voltage spikes, when the voltage jumps up to very high values, or low voltage spikes when the voltage drops low. Spikes are generally of very short duration, sometimes lasting only milliseconds (a millisecond is 1/1000th. of a second), and can have varying effects on electronic equipment.

High voltage spikes are generally caused by equipment such as engine starter motors, electric motors, ignition systems etc, with the starter motors creating the main problems. These spikes are usually of very short duration but can reach levels as high as 300 volts from a 12 volt supply. Low voltage spikes, more correctly called a negative going pulse, are caused by the battery supply being subjected to a very heavy load for a short time, such as when an engine starter motor first cuts in. Negative going pulses are generally of a much longer duration, and the voltage can drop as low as six volts for short periods of time.

High voltage spikes tend to do more permanent damage to electronic equipment, while the low voltage drops tend to play havoc with electronic memories. Most modern equipment, including GPS, is safeguarded to a degree by its own internal protection circuitry, but can still suffer damage from severe spiking. Many unexplained failures of equipment are caused by a constant barrage of high voltage spiking. Components may be able to take spiking for some time, but continual abuse will shorten their life and cause premature failure. Today most equipment consists of a number of printed circuit boards (PCB), these boards are assembled by machine and are almost impossible to repair, which means if one component fails—for any reason—it generally means a replacement board, which can mean big money.

Negative going pulses are seldom associated with component failure, however they can scramble the electronic memory. The highly sophisticated memory of a GPS is used to retain the original calibration setting, the satellite configuration from the last time it was used and all the waypoints that have been entered into storage. Negative going pulses can cause a catastrophic memory failure severe enough to return the unit to its original factory setting, or more subtle effects when only a few numbers may be corrupted. Whatever the effect, the result is usually the same—the whole of the data in the memory has to be checked, and more often than not, re-entered. Sometimes the effect on the equipment is not immediately apparent, and goes unnoticed until a waypoint's location is obviously wrong, or the indicated distance to a selected waypoint is shown as hundreds of miles when you know it is only a couple of miles away. While a negative going pulse seldom causes component breakdown, it creates much frustration and, if they are lost, hours of work re-installing waypoints into the memory.

Remembering spikes, both positive and negative, are caused by Interference by other equipment on the same power supply, the obvious answer is to have a separate power supply for the electronic equipment—a so-called 'dedicated supply'. Fitting a separate battery to only run the GPS and all of the other electronic equipment certainly solves the problem, but like so many things in life it does come with its own problems. While the total amount of current drawn will be generally small, the battery will still need recharging at regular intervals. It is a simple matter to fit a voltmeter to this battery and trickle charge it at home as soon as the voltage shows signs of dropping, but this can be a real pain, and you must remember to put the charger on before the battery drops too low. The battery cannot be directly hooked up to the boat's motor charging system, for this simply connects it back into the loop. While it is possible to connect the electronics battery to the main battery and the charging circuit via a switch, you must remember to open the switch, to isolate the battery, before switching on your equipment. Human nature being what it is, you will eventually forget, and the first time you forget is when the most damage will be done.

ELECTRONICS BATTERY

The simplest method of keeping a special battery, dedicated as a power supply for electronic equipment, fully charged is to use a simple circuit that incorporates a voltage sensitive relay, which only connects the electronics battery into the main battery circuit after the motor has started and supplies charging current to the batteries. (Refer to electronics battery in the Sounder section)

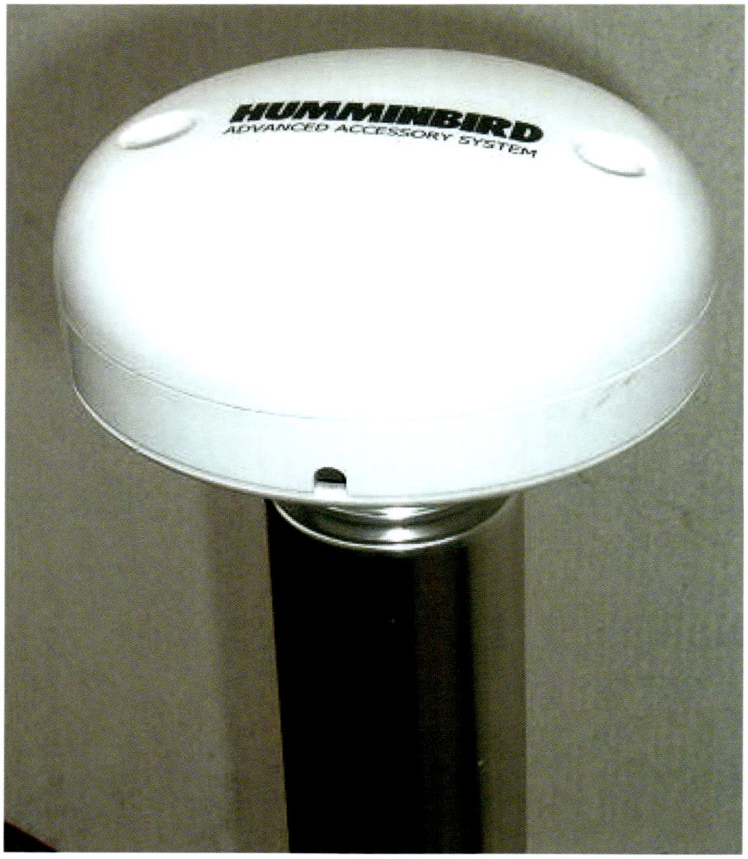

***(Fig 7)* Pole mounted antenna**

GPS pole mounted antenna suitable for mounting on rod racks or for lifting the antenna above obstructions.

Chapter thirteen

The GPS Receiver

The initial GPS receivers were known as navigators and simply provided numerical data such as position, waypoint information etc, however today all units, with the exception of sets for very specialised applications, are plotters. Plotters consist of a number of display screens each of which has a unique function, making up a very powerful navigation tool.

THE PLOTTER SCREEN

The plotter screen represents an area of the earth's surface with the receiver's current position shown in the centre, commonly by a flashing cursor. Imagine the plotter screen to be like a section of a map without any details showing.

The size of the area represented on the screen can be varied from a very large area, typically 300 n miles or more across the screen, down to about 0.1 miles. (The units of measure can be programmed to read in statute miles, (land miles), nautical miles or kilometres. This will be covered in more detail later). The screen can display the position of waypoints, represented by icons or numbers and names, or both. As the boat moves across the plotter screen a track or trail is laid down (sometimes called a 'snail trail'), this is the history of where the boat has been. This track is composed of dots or points, which are joined together to give the appearance of a continuous line.

The GPS has a limited amount of memory for drawing the dots so when all of the memory has been used the unit removes one from the beginning of the track and uses it at the current position. The method by which the track is updated can be varied, it can be laid down at a fixed time interval (generally at one second up to one minute or more) or at a predetermined distance (usually one per 0.01 units of distance to 10 units of distance.) For normal fishing use the shortest update time. All modern units have very large memories, typically 2000 points or more, and when fishing it is rare to run out of track memory. Many units delete the track when switched off or even when plotter scales are changed, however plotter trails can be named and saved in the unit's permanent memory. This is a useful feature; for instance if you have navigated your way out through a tricky channel you may save the track as an aid for navigating the same channel at a later date.

When a waypoint is selected, a dotted line is drawn from the boat's position to the waypoint. If the scale is too small to show the waypoint, the line is extended beyond the edge of the screen.

The plotter screen can be orientated in several ways, North Up, Track Up or Bearing Up. Orientation will be fully dealt with later.

HIGHWAY SCREEN

An alternative to using the plotter for navigating to the destination waypoint, is the Highway display. This is somewhat like a bird's eye view of the boat tracking down a highway towards the waypoint (fig 8). There are almost as many names for this type of display and ways to present this screen as there are manufacturers.

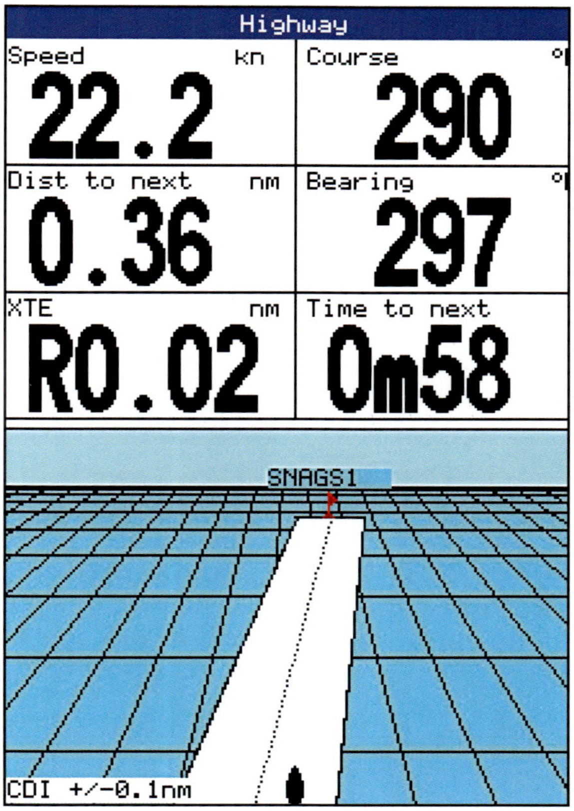

(fig 8) Highway display
Highway or Road screen representing the boats track, or course to the waypoint, the relevant navigation data is displayed at the top of the screen.

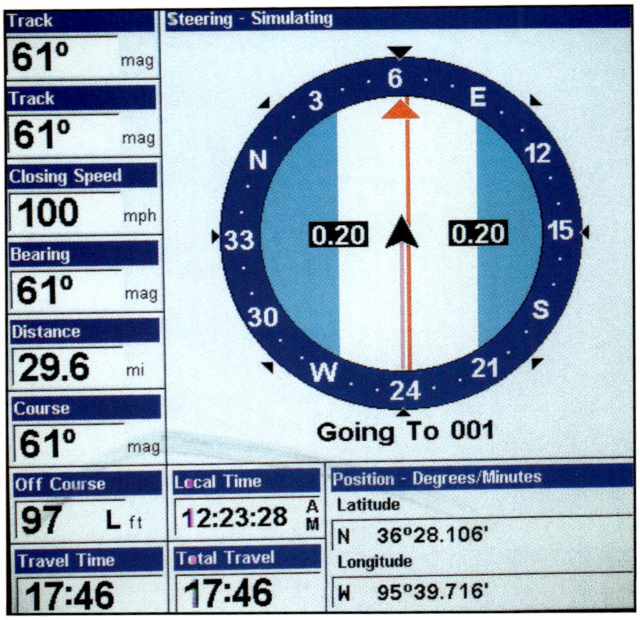

(Fig 9) Compass rose display
Compass rose indicating the boat's track, the road to the waypoint and the compass direction. The navigation data relevant to the waypoint is displayed on the left of the screen.

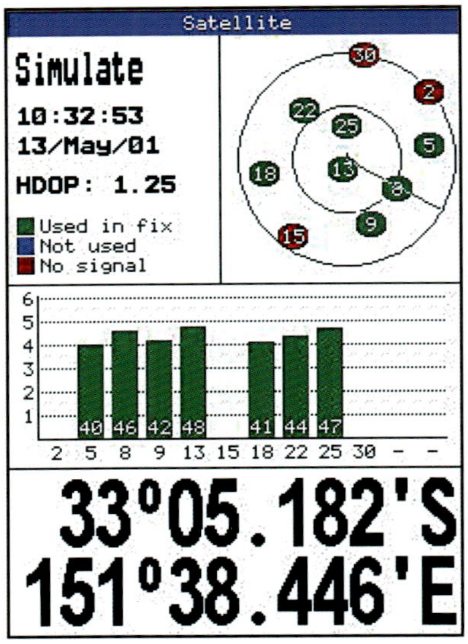

(Fig 10) Satellite display
Satellite status display, indicating the position data for the visible satellites, a graphic representation of their position and signal strength, and the boat's position.

In their latest models Lowrance have a circular display indicating the boat's course surrounded by a compass rose (fig 9), which graphically illustrating the boats direction. The width of the 'road' is the cross track error range. A number of boxes on the left of the screen show the vital navigation data, Humminbird use a unique 3-dimensional view which can be rotated to view the boats progress from any angle, Navman use the classic road presentation which grows shorter as the boat approaches the waypoint.

SATELLITE STATUS SCREEN

This screen displays the functions associated with the satellite data that is being received and processed by the unit. It includes the number of satellites in view of the unit's antenna, the satellites being tracked, which satellites are providing data to the receiver, the signal strength, signal to noise ratio (SNR), the position, time, and the accuracy of the current fix (fig 10). Many of these parameters can be expressed in different ways, depending on the brand of the GPS, again check the owner's manual. The accuracy of the fix in particular can be specified in a number of different ways, American manufactured units (Lowrance, Humminbird) tend to show the error as a distance, that is the error to be expected at the actual location, while units of Japanese origin use the Dilution of Precision (DOP) method, usually the HDOP.

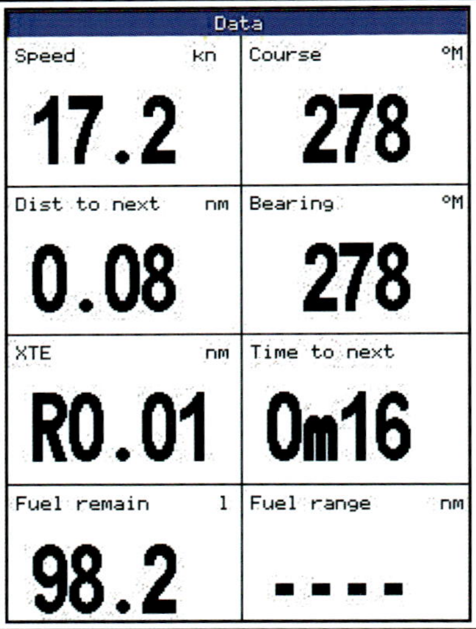

(Fig 11) Data screen
An alternate method of displaying navigation information on the GPS receiver screen.

NAVIGATION DISPLAY

Depending on the brand of plotter, this screen (fig 11) is also called a data display or a position screen. The display typically has a number of large numeric displays indicating important navigation data such as SOG (Speed Over Ground), COG (Course Over Ground), Distance and Bearing to the Waypoint, XTE (Cross Track Error) and TTG (Time To Go). This display is really designed for large vessel operations, particularly when using autopilots, and has very little application for small boats.

CHART PLOTTERS

Chart plotters were a natural progression from GPS plotters. In all respects they are the same as GPS plotters but with the added advantage of being able to

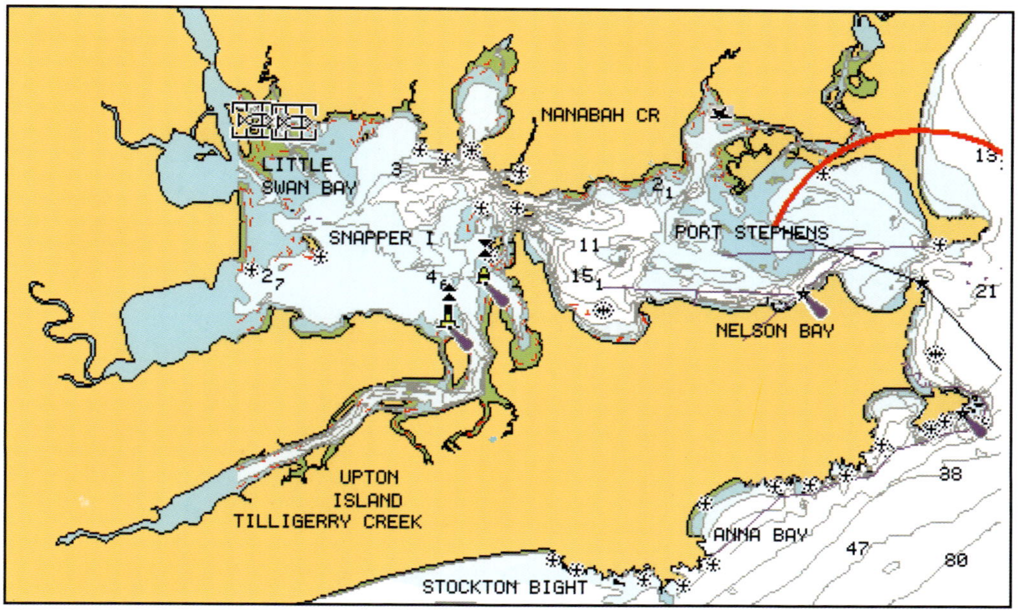

(Fig 12) Chart display
A typical chart display showing navigation information such as depth contours, markers, navigation light arcs etc, boats tracks, courses and waypoints may be overlaid on the chart.

overlay an electronic chart on the screen. Chart plotters have, as standard, a world map installed, however when zoomed-in to useable size the detail is too coarse to be of practical use. To realise the full potential of chart plotters, cartridges are available which contain detailed, up-to-date charts for the Australian coast and offshore waters. The actual area covered by the charts varies from place to place but catalogues are obtainable from the chart suppliers and from GPS dealers.

The chart display can, if necessary, be turned off; the chart plotter then becomes a simple GPS plotter. This may be required in areas that have limited chart coverage and a large degree of zoom is required.

Chart plotters provide another wonderful dimension to GPS receivers, they give informative data on features such as navigation aids, lights, buoys, channel markers, depth contours, safety hazards etc (fig 12). They display waypoint symbols in the correct relationship to landmasses and when a waypoint is selected the bearing line on the chart will indicate if there are any obstructions such as islands or headlands in the course to the destination.

Using a chart of your local area in which you are probably totally familiar may be a case of gilding the lily, however when plying strange waters such as when on holidays or on that voyage of a lifetime they can prove to be priceless. Be wary, while charts have improved dramatically over the last few years, do not trust them implicitly, cross check with admiralty paper charts and heed the warnings with these charts and the warnings in your owners manual.

Another feature is the inclusion of tide and moon phase tables in the chart cards. These tables can be called up (fig 13) for any of the ports included on the chart and display the tidal information for current date. This information is commonly displayed in both numeric and graphic forms, the moon phase and sunrise and sunset times are similarly displayed. If desired the date can be changed to give predictions for other times.

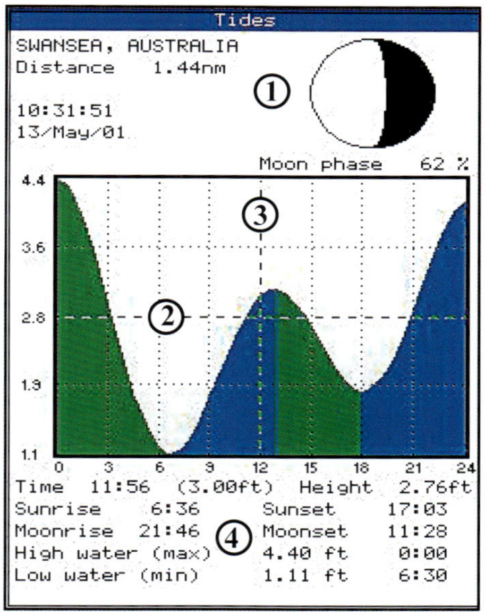

(Fig 13)
Tides and moon
This displays tide and other astronomical information for the port nearest your position. (1) Display the port's name the information refers to, the distance from the boat, the phase of the moon, the current date and time. Then we see (2), height reticules, and (3) is time reticules. Other handy data for the Sun, Moon and tides is shown at (4).

HANDHELD GPS

(Fig 14) Garman handheld GPS

The concept of handheld GPS receivers (fig 14) appeals to a lot of fishermen. They are small, have an in-built antenna, installation is simple (in most cases nothing more than mounting a holding bracket), and they are portable—so if you fish from a mates boat you can take your GPS with you. The greatest disadvantage of the handheld GPS is their size, particularly the screen size. While small handheld screens were once difficult to see, modern screens are brighter and of higher contrast than screens of only a few years ago and are relatively much easier to use. If you have an overriding reason for choosing a handheld unit, such as dual use in bushwalking, shooting etc then the disadvantages when using it in a boat are an acceptable trade-off, however in normal circumstances I would always recommend a full size unit.

As an alternative, data from a handheld receiver can be linked to a full sized plotter via a cable connection. The handheld then becomes, in effect, the plotter's antenna, consequently saving on the cost and giving the user the best of both worlds.

COMBO UNITS

The ideal instrument setup is to have a sounder and a plotter as separate dedicated units, this enables each unit to function independently providing the best possible results from each. However, for reasons of space, or perhaps cost, at times a combination sounder/GPS plotter will be chosen. These combo units, particularly in the larger screen sizes, are ideal for smaller boats and suffer very little in comparison to dedicated units (fig 15).

OFFSETS

Offsets, also called correction factor or map shift, is used to bring the GPS position to correspond with that

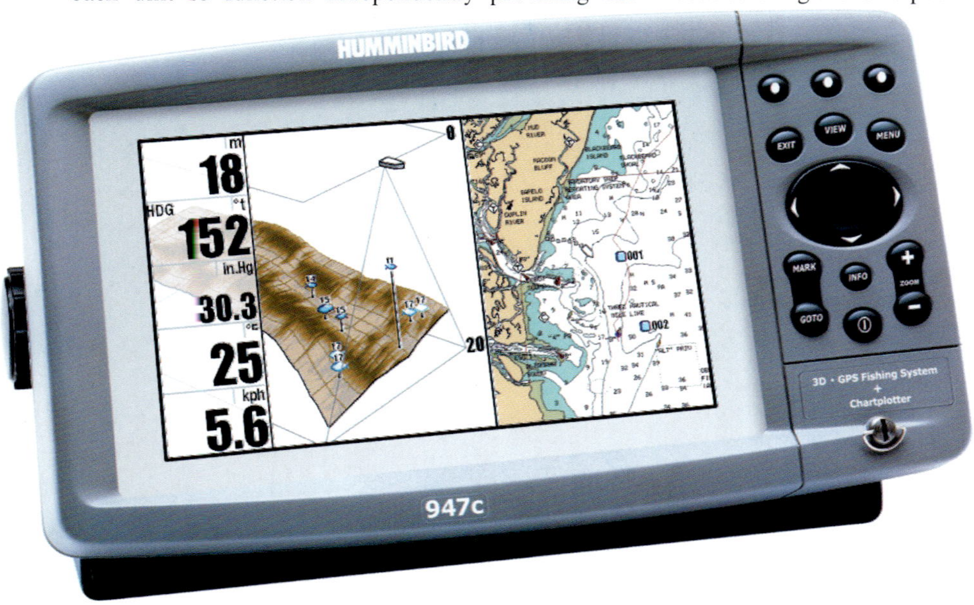

(Fig 15) Combo Chart Plotter and Sounder
Humminbird's 974c combo chart plotter and sounder. The screen is divided into three separate displays, from left to right, numerical data, topographic chart of the bottom and chart.

of a paper chart. For instance, you may regularly use a particular buoy as a turning point, however the physical position of the buoy does not agree with the chart display on your plotter, or the buoy's position plotted on a paper chart. This can be caused by various reasons, such as incorrect chart datum, incorrect original plotting of the buoy, HDOP errors in the system, etc.

Using offsets, which are corrections applied to all latitude and longitude readings within the receiver, it is possible to make the chart display and the GPS agree. Offsets are usually decimal minutes either added or subtracted from the latitude and longitude readings of the GPS receiver. Offsets should be approached with extreme caution. Offsets are actually an intentional error and effect all functions of the GPS, including navigation and recording waypoints. While offsets are a legitimate function of the GPS receiver, they should be given a great deal of thought and consideration before employing them.

Often, if the GPS has been spiked (see Voltage Spikes), it is the offset menu which is corrupted by the addition of error corrections. If your unit has been spiked this is one of the areas of the unit's memory, which should be checked and corrected if found to be corrupted.

WAYPOINT LIST

This screen display contains your library of all your waypoints. Here the list can be sorted into any convenient order, individual entries edited, re-named, re-numbered or deleted. The waypoint list (fig 16) represents many hours of work, either through adding waypoints by latitude and longitude coordinates or by going to the spot. Due to the limited size of the GPS receiver's keyboard, it is a laborious task to enter a large number of waypoints. Many units have the ability to interface with a personal computer (PC) and upload and download data, usually waypoints but specialised charts can also be uploaded from the PC. A full size computer keyboard makes it much quicker to type in the waypoints and then upload them than it would be using the GPS input system.

One very important point, which cannot be over stressed, NEVER TRUST AN ELECTRONIC MEMORY! It is Murphy's Law that sometime, somehow, the memory will fail—be it in a GPS or a computer. Always have some type of backup, be it electronic or hard copy, or both. There is too much time and effort put into a waypoint list to lose it cold, as many have found out over the years.

Depending on the brand and model of the GPS you have purchased, the initialisation, set-up and operation may differ slightly from the descriptions in this text, but a quick check in the owner's manual should tell you what is needed for your particular unit. The owner's manual is a valuable document, take the time to read it and store it in a safe place for reference in the future.

Waypoints

▾Name	Latitude Longitude	DST(nm) BRG(°M)	Dngr Disp
3PTWIDE	33°31.790'S 151°32.422'E	27.2 178	No I+N
8 MILE	33°53.060'S 151°25.853'E	49.1 180	No I+N
9 MILE	33°53.170'S 151°27.599'E	48.9 178	No I+N
AVOCADRP	33°28.580'S 151°27.338'E	25.2 189	No I+N
AVOCAJEW	33°28.320'S 151°27.180'E	25.0 189	No I+N
AVOCAWDE	33°30.050'S 151°32.200'E	25.5 179	No I+N
BAILS	33°43.416'S 151°23.716'E	40.2 185	No I+N
BASS	32°01.739'S 151°03.803'E	69.7 323	No I+N
BIG RED	33°55.360'S 151°24.760'E	51.5 180	No I+N
BIRCHPAR	33°38.305'S 151°22.695'E	35.7 189	No I+N
BOULT0NS	33°36.550'S 151°22.416'E	34.2 190	No I+N
BOULTON1	33°36.610'S 151°22.240'E	34.3 190	No I+N
BOXHEAD	33°29.998'S 151°20.000'E	29.2 199	No I+N

(Fig 16) Waypoint listing

This is a typical waypoint list, showing waypoint names, latitudes and longitudes and bearing and distance to the waypoint from the current position.

Chapter fourteen

Initialisation & Set-Up

INITIALISATION

Initialisation is not strictly necessary for the unit to operate correctly, but it does speed up the first 'fix'. A fix is when the GPS receiver has decoded all the data from the satellites and determined its correct position. If the unit is turned on straight out of the box—this is know as a cold start—the receiver will eventually obtain a fix but this could take as long as 20 minutes. However today this is rare with most initial fixes being obtained in considerably less time. Obtaining a fix is considerably reduced in the future so the procedure is well worth being familiar with.

The first step is to input your current position as latitude and longitude. The dealer may supply this information, or you can take it from a chart, or a mate who has a GPS can give it to you. This data does not need to be absolutely accurate about 100 km is close enough, however it is important to make sure you change the 'N' latitude, which will be displayed for a 'S' to indicate the unit is now operating in the southern hemisphere. Similarly make sure you change the 'W' to 'E' in the longitude setting to program the unit for operating in Australian longitudes. Latitude and longitude is expressed in degrees, minutes and points of a minute (not seconds) e.g. S 32° 57.25 for latitude and E 152°37.52 for longitude or sometimes it may be written, as S 32 57.25 for latitude and E 152 37.52 longitude if the typewriter or printer cannot show the degree sign, also sometimes three decimals places are shown. The actual entry of the position will be straightforward, with menus prompting you when and where to input the data.

The date and time are the next entries to be made. Again, depending on where the unit was manufactured, this could be expressed in different formats. The date may be required in year, month, day sequence (know as YY,MM DD format) or month, day and year (MM,DD,YY) or even the one we use, day, month, year (DD,MM,YY.) The owner's manual will tell you what format is needed. Next comes the time. Again this may be entered as 'UTC' time (basically Greenwich Mean Time), or it may be in local time, which should present no problems as this does not need to be absolutely accurate either. If it is UTC time, on the east coast of Australia time is 10 hours ahead, or 11 hours during daylight saving time, the west coast is 8 hours ahead of UTC. There is one point to keep in mind when working on UTC dates and times, if you are initialising your GPS before 10 a.m., (8 a.m. West Coast), the date you are to enter will be yesterdays date, because 10 a.m. is midnight yesterday in Greenwich. Few GPS receivers have provision for half-hour corrections, so if you are in South Australia or the Northern Territory you will just have to compromise.

All of this may seem confusing, but if you take your time and do one step at a time you should have few problems. One of the most important points to remember, you cannot harm the GPS in any way by pressing the wrong key. If you do enter the wrong data, just go back to the beginning and start over. Normally the initialisation process only needs to be undertaken once, when the unit is new, however if you have not used the unit for longer than three months the almanac will be out of date and the unit will need to update the satellites data—in effect a cold start. Also if you have moved the unit over 100 km from its last fix position, it will cold start. To avoid cold starting a partial initialisation can be performed, only changing any parameters that may have altered, i.e. date or position.

This completes the initialisation and your unit should obtain its first fix in a matter of a minute or less. By accessing the status screen you will be able to see the receiver locate and begin tracking the first satellite, then as it downloads the data other satellites will be selected and tracked and then the unit will establish its initial fix.

SET-UP

Setting-up customises the unit to best suit your needs by programming the receiver with the units of measure you wish to use. Units such as speed units e.g. miles per hour, kilometres per hour or knots, distance units e.g. statute miles, kilometres or nautical miles, compass values, either true or magnetic. Other settings that may require attention are the alarm settings e.g. cross track alarm, arrival alarm and anchor alarm. Most of these options are self explanatory, but for those setting up a GPS for the first time the following may be helpful.

UNITS OF MEASURE

Units of measure will probably be either nautical miles or kilometres. Nautical miles have the advantage of being the same units as measured on a marine chart and have a direct relationship with latitude. One degree of latitude is equal to 60 n miles and one minute of latitude equals one n mile. Kilometres have the advantage of being the units of distance we are most familiar with and have the advantage of easily converting to multiples of metres used in search patterns and anchoring techniques (more about these in the practical sections.) If the unit of distance is set to kilometres, the speed will be kilometres per hour (kph) or if nautical miles it will be knots.

COMPASS HEADINGS

Compass heading would normally be set to magnetic, but if you intend to do a lot of reference work with nautical charts, then true readings may be worth considering.

ALARMS

Alarms have a somewhat limited application for the angler, cross track error (XTE) activates when the boat is off the course to the selected waypoint (fig 17). This alarm is provided mainly for auto pilot operation, when hand steering the helmsman is aware of his course and does not need this feature. The arrival alarm (fig 18) is also autopilot orientated, again the helmsman's knows his position in relationship to the waypoint. If this alarm is used it will continue to sound whenever the boat is within the selected distance of the waypoint and will need to be de-activated as soon as possible after arriving, to save the sanity of the crew. While cross track and arrival alarms have little application for fisherman, the anchor alarm (fig 19) is most useful. Once the boat has settled back onto its anchor this alarm is activated, if the boat drags anchor and moves out from the pre-set zone, the alarm will sound. This alerts the crew that the boat has moved off the mark—a very handy feature, particularly at night.

WAYPOINTS

With the GPS receiver initialised and operating parameters set, the next step is to program some waypoints into the unit. In GPS jargon, waypoints are just another way of saying, 'places I may need to go to'. They are usually fishing spots, entrances to ports and other navigation features. These are entered into the unit's memory as latitude and longitude coordinates.

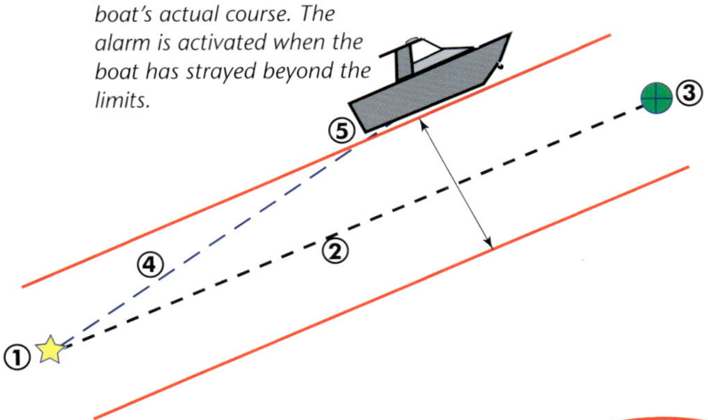

(Fig 17) Off course alarm
(1) Is the starting point, (2) is the bearing to waypoint (3). The red lines parallel to the bearing line are the alarm pre-set limits and (4) is the boat's actual course. The alarm is activated when the boat has strayed beyond the limits.

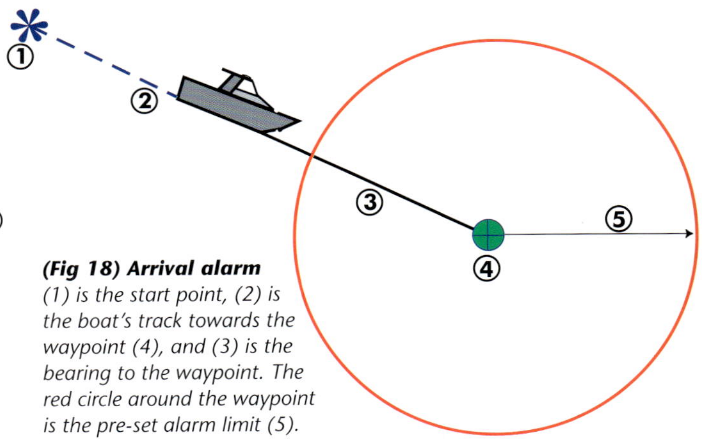

(Fig 18) Arrival alarm
(1) is the start point, (2) is the boat's track towards the waypoint (4), and (3) is the bearing to the waypoint. The red circle around the waypoint is the pre-set alarm limit (5).

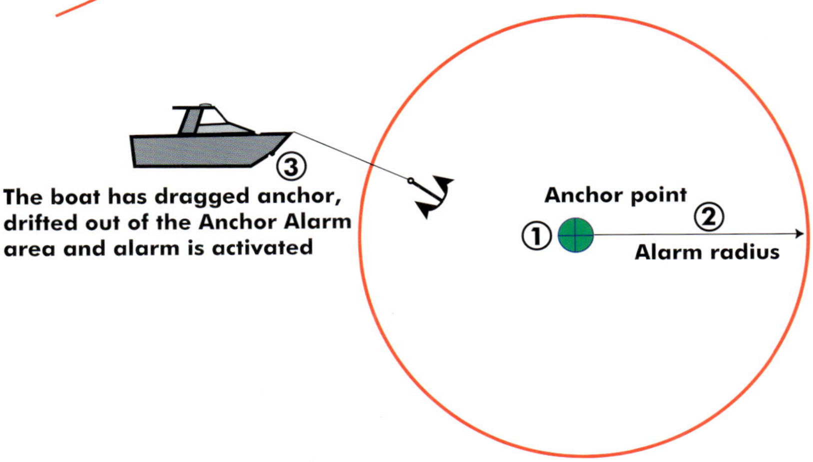

(Fig 19) Anchor alarm
The anchor alarm is the reverse of the arrival alarm. (1) is the boat's position, which was recorded when the boat settled on anchor and (2) is the radius of the pre-set alarm circle. The boat (3) has dragged its anchor and the alarm has sounded.

Chapter fifteen
Practical Applications

ifinder range from Lowrance
Hand held GPS offer a convenient alternative to the fixed GPS

There are several ways to obtain coordinates for your waypoints. Your mates who own GPS will usually give you a set for your local area, (perhaps not their secret spots). Waypoint coordinates are also becoming more common in magazine articles, (Saltwater Sportfishing, Freshwater Fishing Australia) and they are available on the internet at a number of sites, and last but not least you can enter the waypoint into the memory by physically going to the spot.

Assuming you have some waypoint coordinates to enter, access the unit's waypoint memory. Again, this will vary from brand to brand but is usually a prominently marked button, check you manual for details for your set. Once you are into this memory menu, the unit will display a list of waypoints, in our case this will be empty. The first step is to give your waypoint an identification number. While there is no electronic reason you should not give the first waypoint any number you like, it is probably a good move to allocate number one waypoint to the entrance to the port from which you fish the most. It does not matter where you go in a day's fishing, you will always wish to return to the port and if this is number one, it is easiest to remember.

If you have a orderly mind and like to keep everything nice and neat, then allocate blocks of numbers for each port you fish, even separate them into north and south of the port. This keeps all of the locations you are likely to need in a days fishing grouped around the same numbers, making it easier to find a waypoint when you need it. If you choose to enter them in a random fashion, this will have no effect whatsoever on the operation of the unit.

Almost all modern units have a facility to name your waypoints, earlier machines did not have this and it was a pain having to carry a list of your waypoints and their numbers. You will probably be limited to eight letters or numbers with spaces, even though spaces are blank they will still be counted as a letter, but you should have little trouble giving your fishing spots a meaningful name, even with this limitation. Usually the waypoint can be allocated a symbol or icon; this will vary from unit to unit but are self-explanatory. Another feature of modern sets is you will be able to sort the waypoint list, either by name or by number. The choice is entirely up to you. If you have allocated groups of numbers to specific locations then numbers will probably be best, if the waypoints have been entered randomly, alphabetically may be a better way to go. While it is of little importance how you number or sort your waypoint list, it is vitally important you be extremely careful when you are entering the coordinates of a waypoint.

A 'small' error of even a single digit when entering

the data can put you many miles away from the desired spot. Another trap for new players is to overlook the north, south, east and west prefixes. Since all of the GPS available in Australia were designed for sale in the northern hemisphere, they will automatically default to showing an 'N' in the latitude. If you fail to correct this, your waypoint will be many thousands of miles away from where it should be. The longitude prefix may not default to a 'W' reading, the chances are if your set was made in Japan or one of the other Asian countries, it will show 'E' for longitude, however be aware and check and double check your entries.

If your GPS is operating and has given you a fix, it cannot be incorrect (within the limitations of the system). If you call up a waypoint which you know is about five miles away and the display tells you it is hundreds, or even thousands of miles away, it will invariably be operator error and not a faulty unit. If this happens, blame yourself and check the numbers, or better still get somebody else to check. At times you can look at an error a dozen times, and not 'see' it. Another person can come along and pick it up first off. Incorrect data entry has happened to all of use at some time and is part of being human in an electronic world. To correct the error simply go into the edit menu and update it.

CUSTOMISING DISPLAY

During normal day-to-day operation the most common display screen will be the plotter screen, or the 'highway' screen. Both of these screens illustrate, in graphic form, the progress of the boat towards the selected waypoint. These screens can display data boxes, which contain important facts about the navigation status of the GPS (fig 20). Data such as speed over ground (SOG), bearing (to waypoint), distance (to waypoint), course over ground (COG), cross track error (XTE), time to go (to waypoint at current speed) (TTG), latitude and longitude (current position), time of day etc. The number, position and the data displayed in these boxes can be customised to suit your individual taste. My choice is to keep the boxes to a minimum to see more of the plotter screen, using only the important data e.g. speed over ground, bearing, course over ground and distance.

While this chapter is about using your GPS as a general navigation tool, particular emphasis has been placed on the needs of fishermen and the use of techniques to enhance the operation of the system in everyday fishing situations. Most of these practical methods have been developed out on the water fishing during the last fifteen years or so.

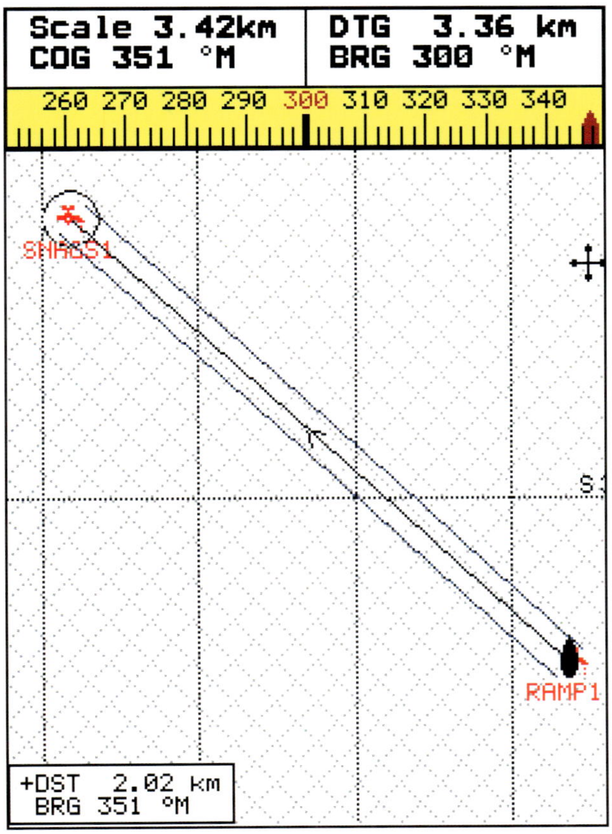

(Fig 20) Customised display

There are numerous ways the display screens can be personally customised to show data important to the operator. In this case the boxes along the top of the plotter display indicate the chart's scale, the current course expressed as magnetic degrees, the distance to the waypoint and the bearing, also in magnetic degrees.

The yellow band below the information boxes is a graphic compass display that indicates the bearing to the waypoint (300 degrees) and the boat's course (351 degrees). The information box at the bottom of the chart display repeats the important information of the distance to the waypoint and the bearing. This illustration also shows a GOTO waypoint being used to navigate to the waypoint 'snags1' from the starting point, 'ramp 1'. The lines on either side of the bearing line indicate the scale set for the 'off course' alarm.

Chapter sixteen

Practical GPS Fishing

RECORDING WAYPOINTS

Entering waypoints by using latitude and longitude coordinates has been covered in detail in a previous chapter but waypoints can also be entered at the actual spot. Most units have a simple, one key stroke operation for storing the current location as a waypoint, the name and procedure varies from brand to brand—refer to the instruction manual for details of your unit. Once you are over the spot you wish to record, simply press the waypoint key and a notice will appear on the screen notifying you that the waypoint has been saved along with its memory location and number. While it is quite practical at this time to go into the waypoint edit menu and give the spot a meaningful name, this job is much easier when the boat is back on the trailer or in the marina. Keep in mind that if you enter more than a couple of waypoints, it pays to jot down a brief description and the number, otherwise when the time comes to edit and name the waypoints it can be difficult remembering the order in which they were recorded.

A method I have found useful, particularly when recording reef areas rather than single isolated points, is to place a mark on the plotter screen as soon as the sounder indicates the start of the reef. A mark, as distinct from a waypoint, is a symbol placed on the plotter screen. The mark is stored in the unit's memory, but unlike a waypoint, which can be named, moved around in the memory and called-up as a destination to go to, marks can only be displayed on the screen and are primarily designed as a temporary indicator. They are stored in a memory and will remain on the plot (even if the unit is switched off) until such times as you physically remove them. By placing a mark on the screen you give yourself a reference point to work around to survey the reef. As I sound over the reef, I place a mark on any significant feature. Later I will convert one of these marks to a waypoint for the reef. If the reef complex is large I will use two waypoints to mark both ends of the reef.

The boat should be stopped, or at least only moving slowly, when saving a waypoint. Even though the update time on modern GPS receivers is one second, if the boat is travelling at an appreciable speed the actual spot recorded could be some distance away from the spot when you pressed the waypoint save key. If the saved waypoint were of a large area like a reef, this would be of little consequence, but if it is a tiny spot, it could be significant. This is particularly so if you are recording waypoints of buoys or channel markers to be used in a route sequence to navigate a narrow channel.

MAN OVER BOARD

One of the most frightening incidents that can happen on a boat is to lose a crewman overboard. Without exception, all GPS receivers have a man over board (MOB) feature, which is generally activated by single keystroke, and places a special waypoint in the memory. Once MOB is in operation, all normal navigation functions are suspended, Goto, Bearing, DTG etc all refer to the spot in the water where the key was pressed. If the MOB key is pressed again, all the data is changed to refer to the new MOB waypoint. Depending on the unit, the MOB function must be cancelled before normal navigation can be resumed.

GOTO WAYPOINT

To call up a waypoint to go to is generally no more complex than finding the waypoint in the unit's memory, highlighting it and selecting the Goto command. If you are using the plotter screen the boat's position will be shown in the centre of the screen and a dotted line will extend to the waypoint (fig 20) if the map's scale is sufficiently large to cover the waypoint's position. If the scale is not sufficiently large the line, called the bearing line, will disappear off the side of the screen. The data boxes at the bottom of the screen will show the distance to the waypoint (DTG) and the bearing (in compass degrees).

When I call up a waypoint I adjust the scale to show the selected waypoint, that is if the DTG display indicates 8.5 n mile, the scale would be 20 n mile This enables me to check that I have called up the right number for the waypoint and the waypoint is about where it should be, and has thus been entered correctly. When I start to navigate to the location, I will bring the scale back to 5 n mile, which I find is a comfortable range to travel on. Once the boat is tracking down the dotted bearing line, I look ahead and try and find a point towards which to steer the boat. If the land is in sight this is easy, but if there is only sea, I may use a convenient cloud, if there are no clouds then I take note of the direction the sea is meeting the boat and use this to steer by. At night I choose a star. Every few minutes check your progress on the plotter and make any adjustments to your aiming point. This is much easier than attempting to steer directly from the plotter screen alone or by the compass.

When the DTG display indicates 0.5 n mile slow the boat to sounding speed and check that the sounder settings are right for the depth. Change the plotter screen to the largest magnification, usually 0.1 n mile, and warn the crew to have the anchor ready, and by this time you should be just about ready to pass over the waypoint. On their latest models, Lowrance have an auto zoom feature which, when a waypoint is selected, adjusts the plotter scale (zooms out) until the whole of the course is visible, from the present position to the waypoint. As the boat moves the unit automatically zooms in, always keeping the waypoint on the screen but always at the maximum scale size.

The alternate method of navigating to a waypoint is to use the highway screen.

GPS COMPASS

The GPS receiver has no in-built compass. Compass readings are generated by the unit knowing where it was a second ago and where it is now and thus the direction the boat has moved to reach this position. It is important to realise a GPS compass reading indicates which direction the boat is moving, a compass indicates which direction the boat is pointing. At very low speed the GPS compass can be misleading and in conditions of strong cross winds or current there may be a discrepancy between the two systems (fig 21).

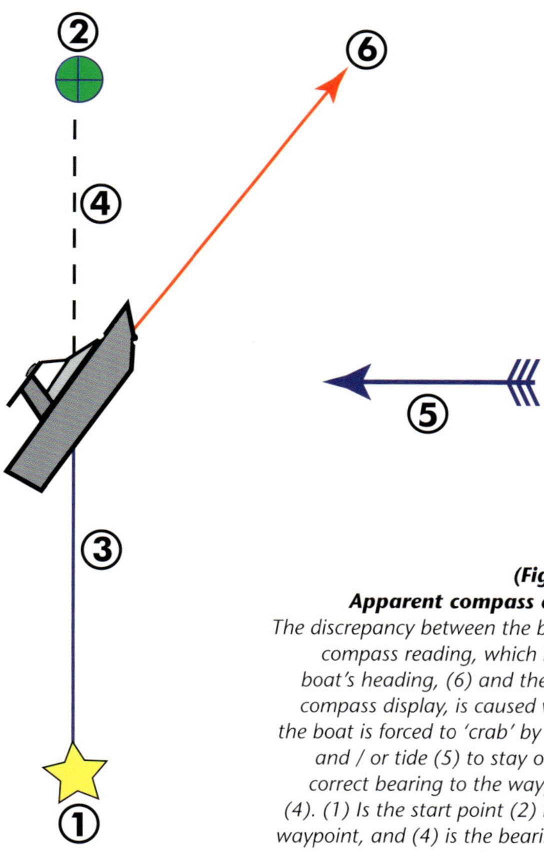

(Fig 21) Apparent compass error

The discrepancy between the boat's compass reading, which is the boat's heading, (6) and the GPS compass display, is caused when the boat is forced to 'crab' by wind and / or tide (5) to stay on the correct bearing to the waypoint (4). (1) Is the start point (2) is the waypoint, and (4) is the bearing to the waypoint

ROUTES

Routes, sometimes called a 'route sequence', are a string of waypoints linked together to mark a course of travel (fig 22). Routes have been likened to a string of beads, the beads representing the waypoints and the string representing the course connecting waypoint to waypoint. In GPS jargon the course from one waypoint to the next is a 'leg' and routes are composed of any number of legs. The legs are based on straight lines between waypoints. This is an important fact to keep in mind whenever dealing with routes.

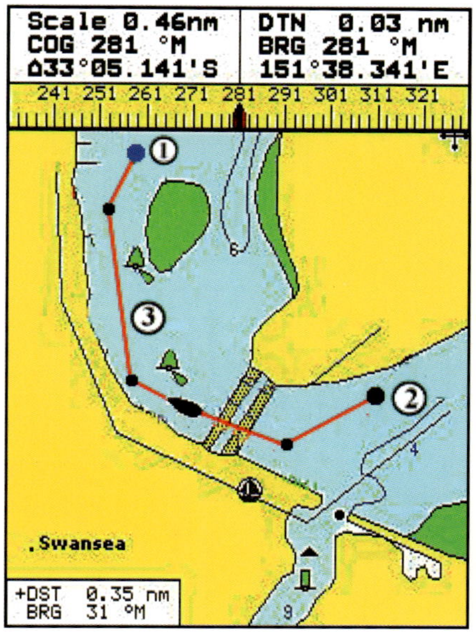

(Fig 22) Routes

A route is a group of waypoints linked together to navigate a pre-set course. The illustration is a route down the narrow Swansea Channel. (1) is the end point, (2) is the starting point and (3) is the course to navigate through the channel. This is a relatively short route to illustrate the princi-ple, in reality the route would extend from the Heads to the end of the channel.

Routes provide the automatic capability to navigate through a number of waypoints without having to program the GPS each time a waypoint is reached, when the boat arrives at a waypoint the GPS automatically selects the next waypoint in the sequence. Routes are stored in the memory, usually under a name or a number, often both, and can be navigated forward through the group or in the reverse order, also you can start navigating, either forward or back from any point in the sequence.

Routes are a very powerful feature of GPS plotters, providing a means of easy progress through tricky navigation situations, such as narrow channels etc. and makes long trip planning a breeze. Routes can be created by several methods, travelling along the planed course and making waypoints at each point it is necessary to change the boat's direction, from a list of waypoints already stored in the plotter's memory or from the chart display on the plotters screen. If you elect to create a route using the plotter chart display and the route is through some narrow waters or among obstructions, it is worthwhile checking the route under good conditions to verify its accuracy.

A few points to keep in mind about routes are first, always confirm that any leg does not cross land or dangerous waters. Second, any waypoint can be used in a route and can be used more than once in that route and using a waypoint in a route sequence does not preclude it from being used in normal navigation. Third, while it is possible to skip a waypoint when travelling along a route, be very careful if you do so, as this action may change the whole complexion of the route and give rise to a dangerous situation.

Routes can be a little fiddling to set-up but are well worth the effort, such as when you have to find your way back into harbour on a dark, wet night.

PLOTTER ORIENTATION

The plotter screen may be orientated in several ways, north-up, track-up or course-up. North-up is usually the default orientation (fig 23), that is north is always at the top of the plotter screen, just as it is in paper charts and

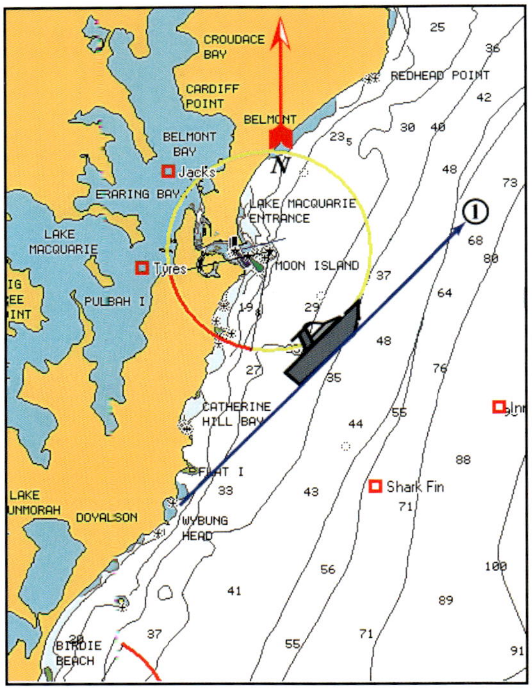

(Fig 23)
North Up chart orientation
The chart is always shown with the North at the top of the screen and the bearing to the waypoint is shown with its true relationship to North.

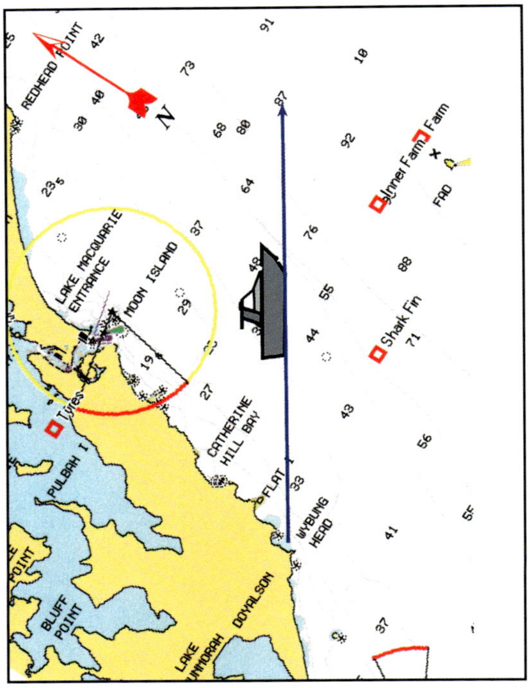

(Fig 24)
Head Up chart orientation
The chart is rotated to always show the boat's heading at the top of the screen. North Up and Head Up do not require a waypoint to be selected to function.

maps. When you are navigating to a waypoint which is to the north, everything is fine, if you drift off to the left of the bearing line just move to the right and you come back on course. In other words what you see on the left side of the screen is on your left, and so on. However when travelling on any other bearing, the plotter screen no longer agrees with your view of the world. If for example your are travelling south and drift off course to the left and you adjust by bringing the boat back to the right, the error will increase. The trick is not to think as left and right but as compass directions. If, when moving north the error is to the left, it is actually to the west and is corrected by moving to the east, similarly when moving south and the error is to the left, it is actually to the east and a westerly correction is required. This may, at first, sound complicated but your mind will quickly adapt and the correction becomes almost automatic.

To overcome this problem many of the modern plotters have a track-up mode (fig 24), which rotates the display to keep the top of the plotter in the direction the boat is moving, thus left is left etc. Another alternative is course-up orientation (fig 25), which presents the bearing to the waypoint always at the top of the screen. (Of course, a waypoint must be selected for this orientation to operate).

I have found the track-up mode to be somewhat disconcerting with the plotter screen re-positioning every time the boat's heading changes, even if it is only a slight change in direction. Course-up is an excellent orientation, particularly for new users who have difficulty coming to grips with the traditional north-up orientation. (This is the orientation that Highway displays use).

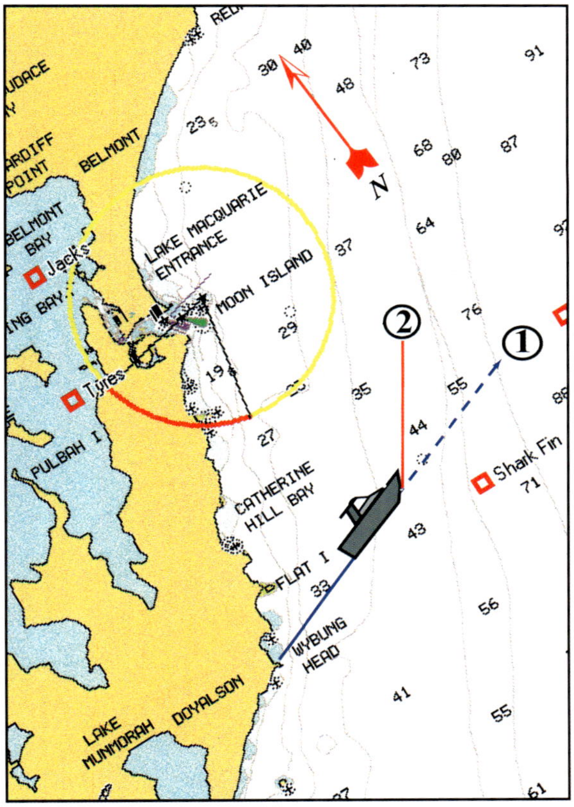

(Fig 25) Course Up orientation

The chart is oriented to show the bearing to the waypoint at the top of the screen. To function, a waypoint must be selected.

PRACTICAL ACCURACY

Accuracy theory of the GPS system was covered earlier, however there are other factors that effect accuracy that you can expect from your unit in the field. These are defined as 'repeatable accuracy' and 'relative accuracy'. Repeatable accuracy is the precision that can be expected when the GPS is navigating back to a waypoint that has been created by that particular unit. This is usually totally accurate within the limits of the system. Relative accuracy refers to the degree of accuracy, which can be expected from waypoints made with other units or coordinates from charts. Earlier GPS units, due to component tolerances, could exhibit latitude and longitude reading errors as great as 100 metres. Modern units have closer component tolerances and use improved software, which has improved accuracy to a few metres. Another point to keep in mind when using waypoint lists is that many of these waypoints were recorded when S/A was operating and these will contain the inherent positional errors of that system.

SEARCH PATTERNS

Even with the vastly improved accuracy there will be occasions when you will need to search for the correct location. If, after running down your selected waypoint, and accurately passing through the waypoint symbol on the plotter screen, the sounder does not show the spot you are looking for, then a pattern search should be undertaken. While it is easy and human nature to just have a quick look around the mark to see if you can find it, this usually leads to wandering all over the place and creating snail tracks all over the screen, and still not finding the spot. Then once a proper pattern search is used the spot shows up, not all that far away. Take my word for it, I have done it. A search is easy to implement and will quickly put you bang onto the spot; however here are a few facts that will make understanding a pattern search quite a little easier.

The first factor to keep in mind is the area of bottom your echo sounder is covering. Unless you are in very deep water you will probably be using a 20 degree cone angle transducer which covers an area about one third of the depth. Supposing the depth of water over the selected waypoint is 30 metres, the sounder will be sounding a 10 metre circle, which as the boat moves along will become a ten metre wide strip, five metres either side of the boat's track. Now take into consideration the probable error of the fix, if it is a location from a waypoint list or from another unit it could be as bad as 100 metres. Bearing all of this in mind, if you do a grid pattern search, with each leg about 20 metres apart, and 50 metres long you will cover the possible location of the spot in a maximum of six or seven legs (fig 26), in practice, usually a lot less. This theoretical case assumes you will sweep the bottom with your sounder, with the possibility of missing any one spot by a maximum of five metres. However since the spot you are looking for is unlikely to be that small and, in practice, the transducer's beam wanders over a much wider area than theory suggests, due to wave motion rocking the boat from side to side. This search method works extremely well in practice.

To start the search pattern just continue on the course you were using to get to the waypoint, travelling through the waypoint icon by about 50 metres. The obvious question is how far is 50 metres on the plotter screen? If you are using nautical miles for distance measurements and knots for speed then a rule-of-thumb type of calculation assumes a nautical mile is 2,000 metres, 0.1 n mile is then 200 metres and 0.01 n mile is twenty metres. Remember these simple figures for you will find them very handy in doing a number of quick calculations on the water in a day's fishing. If you are using kilometres then the calculations are even simpler. But back to our search pattern, what you must do now is to work out what an actual measurement on the screen represents in metres on the water. Measure the plotter screen in millimetres, just the actual plotter screen, do not include the area covered by the information boxes. For this example, suppose the screen is 100 mm by 100 mm, and we are using a scale of 0.25 n mile. It is simple arithmetic to work out 0.25 n mile (500 metres) equal 100 mm or 5 metres equals 1 mm on the screen. So on this scale of 0.25 n mile, 50 metres would be represented on the plotter screen by 10 millimetres. Had the scale been 0.1 n mile, (200 metres), 50 metres would be represented by 25 millimetres.

While all of this may seem a little complicated you only need to do it once and then remember it, or better still, jot it down in your marks book for future reference. If you always use the same scale it quickly becomes second nature to estimate distance on the screen. I always use 0.25 n mile scale for my close searching work, and I know that 10 mm represents about 50 metres on the screen. Humminbird's latest models, Matrix models 55 and 65, have a grid feature, which can be overlaid on the waypoint, this is called a trolling grid and makes setting up a search pattern simplicity itself. Once the spot is located record it as a waypoint and then when you have the time replace the original one with the new, corrected one.

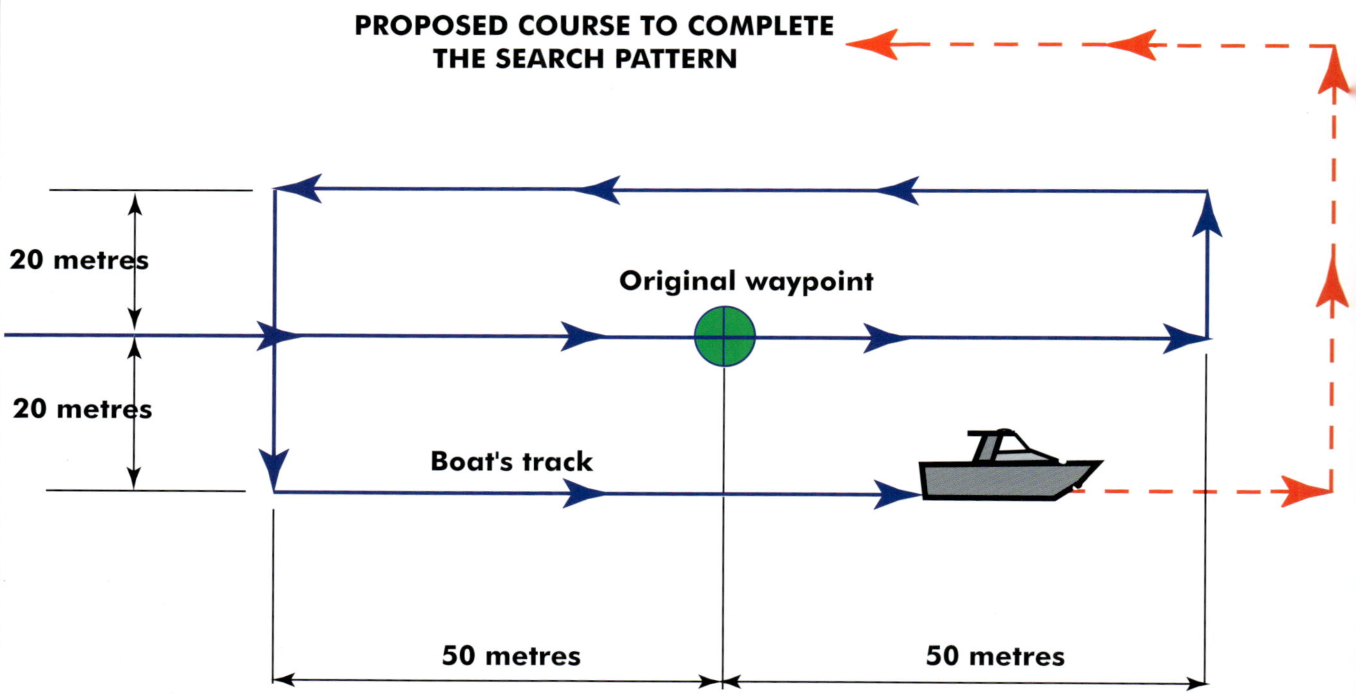

(Fig 26)
Search pattern
A method of carry out a systematic search using the GPS and sounder to locate a feature on the bottom. For a full description of performing such a search, refer to the text.

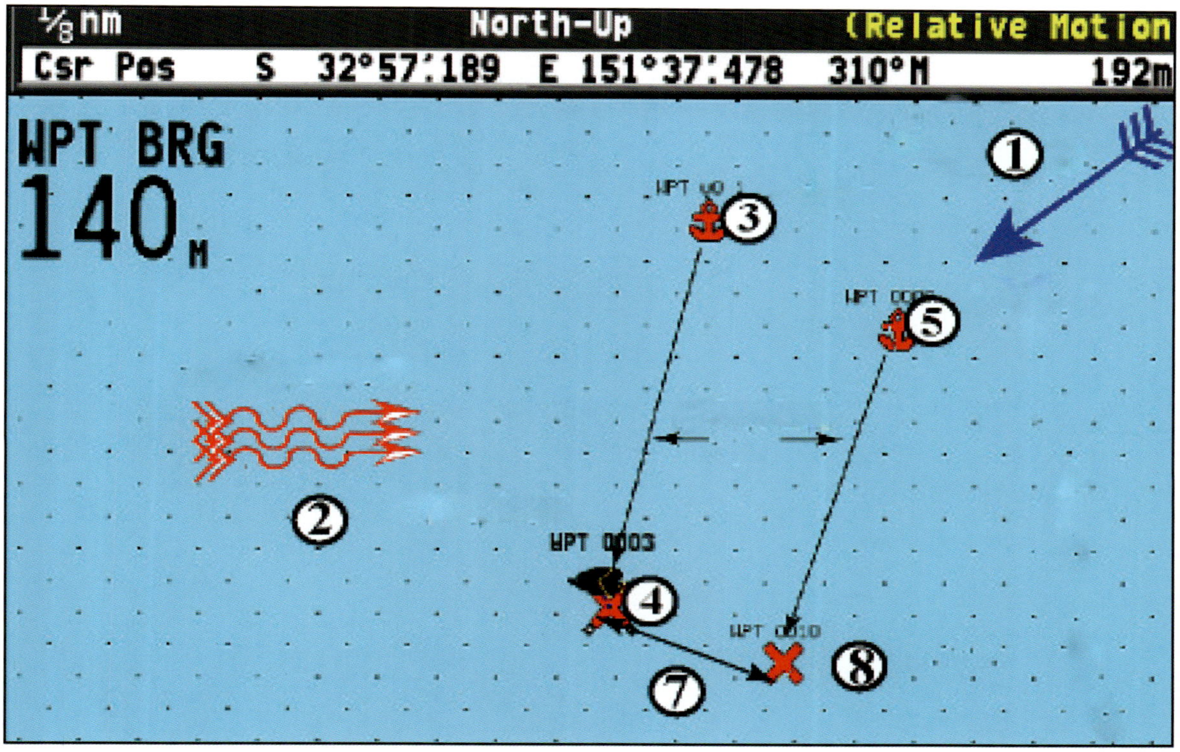

GPS ANCHORING

The DTG and BRG displays are handy for those occasions when, after locating the fishing spot, you have anchored but have not laid over the spot you wish to fish, because of current or wind, or a combination of both. Once you have settled on the anchor, check the displays, the DTG will tell you how far off the spot you are, and the BRG will tell you in which direction it is. Often, from this data, it is possible to swing the boat over to the spot, or if you must go and re-anchor, you will have a pretty good idea what correction needs to be made as to where to drop the pick. On occasions, particularly when anchoring in deep water, another more sophisticated method needs to be employed. The illustration (fig 27) is explained in the caption. This plot was made in a depth of 100 metres off Swansea on the NSW central coast. The first screen shows the boat's position after it has laid back on the anchor. Due to the unknown direction and strength of the current when the anchor was first dropped, the boat has finished about 180 metres off the mark. While this may seem a large distance, errors of this magnitude are common in deep water when there is up to 300 metres of anchor rope in the water. The distance and the direction the boat is out of position are used to estimate the point where the anchor should be re-positioned. This system is simple and quite accurate and saves a lot of time and effort in deepwater fishing.

(Fig 27) GPS anchoring
The factors effecting the boat's position when it lies back on its anchor are wind (1) and / or current (2). (8) is the waypoint selected to fish, (3) is the position the anchor was first dropped and (4) the boat's position when it came up on the anchor, approximately 180 metres (7) off the waypoint (8). Using the distance and the direction the boat was off the spot as a guide, the anchor was retrieved and dropped at (5) and this time settled back right over the waypoint.

Chapter seventeen

The Future

While it is a risky business trying to prophesise the future path of marine electronics, (as I have found out in the past), it is a pretty fair bet to expect integration to play a big large part of that future. Today a number of the major manufacturers have already started on that path with tide and moon predictions an integral part of chart plotters, fuel flow meters are available, as well as barometric displays and radar images overlaid onto chart displays are now available. Engine monitoring displays incorporated into plotters are now standard on many plotters and as the price of colour screens fall, we will see more and more colour used in the cheaper price-ranged units. More data is being stored into smaller and smaller packages. As an example look at the size of the current electronic chart chips, smaller than a postage stamp (fig 28) and yet containing more data than the old cards of only a few years ago which were three times the size. Data exchange between units and home computers, (PC's), already available on some models will become more commonplace, as will navigation data available on the Internet. Whatever happens in the future, it will be an exciting time for users of Global Position System.

(Fig 28) Data storage
Size comparison of SD (Secure Digital) cards to a postage stamp. These cards are now capable of storing gigabytes of date and are becoming cheaper by the day.

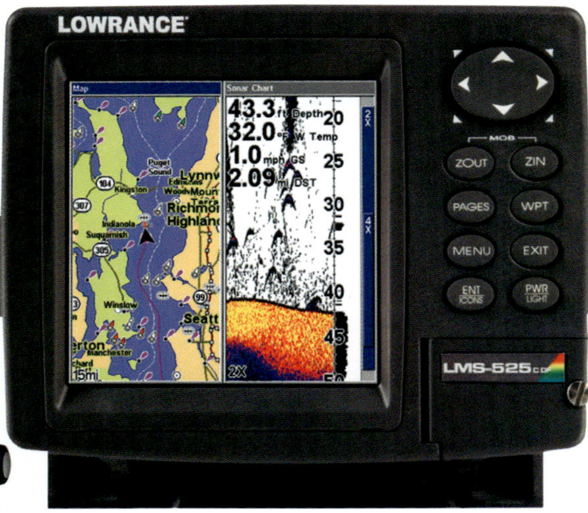

Lowrance 525
Lowrance's 525c sounder plotter typical of the state of the art sounder/chart plotters.

Raymarine
Raymarine's display units are capable of integrating with a range of units such as sounders, radar, GPS chart plotters etc, displaying the images in various combinations of split screen.

Glossary

AGD66	Australian Geodetic Datum 66 (see Datum.)
AGD84	Australian Geodetic Datum 84 (see Datum.)
BRG	Compass Bearing to the destination waypoint.
CDI	Course Deviation Indicator. The distance the boat has deviated from the straight line course to the waypoint. Also called Cross Track Error (XTE.)
Chart card	A plug-in card which stores chart data for an area.
Chart datum	see Datum.
COG	Course Over Ground. The compass direction the boat is moving over the ground, not necessarily the direction it is pointing.
CTS	Course To Steer. The optimum compass course to steer to bring the boat back to the plotted course to the waypoint.
Cursor	A symbol on the display screen indicating the entry position or the boat's position.
Datum	A fixed, geodetic, point on the earth's surface against which all other positions are measured for drawing maps and charts. World Geodetic System (WGS84) will slowly replace all other systems (see also AGD Australian Geodetic Datum 66 and 84).
DD,MM,YY	Day, Month, and Year date format.
DGPS	Differential Global Positioning System. A supplementary navigation system to correct errors in the GPS.
DOP	Dilution of Precision. A measure of the quality of a satellite configuration and its effect on the accuracy of the fix (see also HDOP Horizontal Dilution Of Precision).
DTG	Distance To Go the distance from the boat's present position to the waypoint.
EGNOS	European Geostationary Navigation Overlay Service. The European system of DGPS using satellites as well **as base**
GOTO	A simple method of navigating to a waypoint.
GPS	Global Positioning System. A global navigation system based on a satellite constellation.
HDOP	Horizontal Dilution of Precision. A length and breadth measurement of satellite configuration and its effect on accuracy of the fix (see also DOP Dilution of Precision.)

HF	High Frequency. Radio frequencies used to transmit Differential Global Positioning System (DGPS) data (see also VHF Very High Frequency and UHF Ultra High Frequency.) Leg The straight segments of a route between waypoints. A route with four waypoints will have three legs.
LOP	Line of Position are used in all types of navigation and refer to a number of points, including position, which lie in a straight line.
MM,DD,YY	Month, Day and Year date format.
MOB	Man Over Board. A function that starts navigating back to the spot where the person fell overboard.
NMEA	National Marine Electronics Association (United States.)
NMEA0183	A standard for interfacing marine electronic devices.
Offset	Also called, correction factor or map shift, is used to bring the GPS position to correspond with that of a paper chart.
PRN	Pseudo-Random Number. A method of numbering GPS satellites. (see RouteTwo or more waypoints linked in sequence to form a course for the boat to automatically follow.
SNR	Signal to Noise Ratio A measure of radio signal strength compared to background noise.
SOG	Speed Over Ground. The boat's speed over the ground, which may not be the boat's speed through the water because of current, wind etc.
SVID	Space Vehicle Identity a method of numbering GPS satellites (see also PRN Pseudo-Random Number.)
TTG	Time To Go. The estimated time to reach the waypoint at current speed (see also ETA Estimated Time of Arrival.)
UHF	Ultra High Frequency. Radio frequencies used to transmit Differential Global Positioning System (DGPS) data (see also VHF Very High Frequency and HF High Frequency.)
UTC	Universal Time Coordinated which is the standard world time (formally known as Greenwich Mean Time (GMT).
VHF	Very High Frequency. Radio frequencies used to transmit Differential Global Positioning System (DGPS) data (see also UHF Ultra High Frequency and HF High Frequency .)
WAAS	Wide Area Augmentation System. An American system of DGPS using satellites as well as base stations (see **also EGNOS** European Geostationary Navigation Overlay Service.)
Waypoint	A user-defined navigation location store in the GPS Receiver's Memory.
XTE	Cross Track Error. The distance the boat has deviated from the direct course to the waypoint (see also CDI Course Deviation Indicator.)
YY,MM,DD	Year, Month and Day date format.